*Select the perfect wines for
every occasion with*

THE CONCISE
WINE GUIDE

- Choose appropriate wines for dinners, parties, quiet evenings at home

- Compare wines of all types and pick a winner every time

- Find quality wines at affordable prices

- Enjoy a variety of domestic and imported wines

- Know the best wine vintages

  . . . AND MUCH MORE!

THE CONCISE WINE GUIDE

Shelagh Ryan Masline

Produced by
The Philip Lief Group, Inc.

BERKLEY BOOKS, NEW YORK

THE CONCISE WINE GUIDE

A Berkley Book / published by arrangement with
The Philip Lief Group, Inc.

PRINTING HISTORY
Berkley edition / February 1993

All rights reserved.
Copyright © 1993 by The Philip Lief Group, Inc.
Produced by The Philip Lief Group, Inc.,
6 West 20th Street, New York, New York 10011.
This book may not be reproduced in
whole or in part, by mimeograph or any other
means, without permission. For information
address: The Berkley Publishing Group,
200 Madison Avenue, New York, New York 10016.

ISBN: 0-425-13633-7

A BERKLEY BOOK ® TM 757,375
Berkley Books are published by The Berkley Publishing Group,
200 Madison Avenue, New York, New York 10016.
The name "BERKLEY" and the "B" logo
are trademarks belonging to Berkley Publishing Corporation.

PRINTED IN THE UNITED STATES OF AMERICA

10   9   8   7   6

To my daughter Caitlin,
whose birth occasioned
the most special Champagne toast
of my lifetime.

Acknowledgments

Thanks to my editors at the Philip Lief Group, Eva Weiss and Julia Banks. And great thanks also to my wonderful mother, Eileen, and brother Timmie, for the unfailing love, support, hot meals and warm nest they provide for me and my daughter.

Thanks also to Bob Hernandez for his thoughtful professional review of the manuscript.

Contents

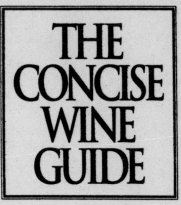

THE CONCISE WINE GUIDE

Introduction

In a busy world it's important to take time out for the relaxing pleasures of civilized eating and drinking with family and friends.

For some, a bottle of wine makes a perfect addition to a festive meal. Others regard a glass of wine with dinner as a treasured ritual. We entertain our guests with wine at special dinners, whether at home or in a restaurant. At large parties, jug wines and wine punch seem just the thing. Wine can enhance any romantic evening, and bring warmth to a table shared with good friends and loved ones.

The Concise Wine Guide will lead you through the shelves of wine in a liquor store, and the many choices of a wine list, to select the wines that best suit your own taste and budget. You'll learn how wine is made and what to look for in the different types of wine. If at any point a term is unfamiliar, refer to the Glossary at the end of the book.

Also offered here are practical tips on which wines best complement a wide range of foods. In the summer, for example, it's time for a cool, light and refreshing wine to accompany your salad; while in winter you can hunker down with a hearty red wine and a piping hot stew. Save a glass to drink curled up on the couch with a good book or your favorite TV show.

We'll take a tour of wines around the world: from those in our own backyard, to the famous—and not so famous—wines of France, to more wines of Europe, Australia and South America. Flip back to the Index of Common, Economical and Tasteful Wines, and you'll find a wide array of wines available from all these countries—for $10 and under!

How do the experts taste wine? Now you can learn how to "chew" your wine with the best of them. If all this has inspired you to begin your own wine collection, we'll tell you how to go about it in Chapter Nine.

And if you'd like to rummage through your wine collection to entertain your friends, look for helpful hints on the styles and amounts of wine it is appropriate to serve on various occasions.

There are no hard and fast rules here—only simple guidelines that will enable you to sit back, relax and savor your entry into the wonderful world of wine.

One

From Cask to Flask: How Is Wine Made?

To begin with, let's find out how wines are made. How, for example, does a winemaker create a still or sparkling wine? What are the basic components of wine? What factors go into determining the quality of a wine?

Read this chapter carefully to learn the answers to these and other questions. You will find the information here invaluable background for the chapters that follow.

What Is Wine?

Wine is basically fermented grapes. When grape juice is fermented, it becomes wine.

What Are the Basic Components of Wine?

The basic recipe for wine is sugar + yeast = alcohol + carbon dioxide.

Sugar is a substance present naturally in ripe grapes. Yeast is present naturally on grape skins. Modern winemakers, however, often prefer to use their own specially prepared yeasts, in order to exercise more control over the final product.

Yeast causes sugar to convert into alcohol. The fermentation process is complete when all the sugar has been transformed into alcohol or the wine reaches an alcoholic content of 15 percent. This in turn destroys the yeast.

Carbon dioxide is a by-product of the fermentation process. In the case of still wines, carbon dioxide is allowed to evaporate into the air. In sparkling wine it is preserved.

When Are Grapes Harvested?

Grapes are harvested when the winemaker decides that they have reached the balance of sugar and acid appropriate to the style of wine he or she desires to produce. After harvest, grapes are first destemmed, then crushed and pressed in a vatting shed. Their juice is collected in tanks or barrels to ferment.

How Is Wine Aged?

Traditionally wine was aged and fermented in wood. Today, however, wines are also often aged in stainless-steel tanks, glass-lined tanks or cement tanks. Some wines also benefit from bottle-aging.

When wine is aged in wood, flavor and tannins are added to the wine. The younger the wood, the more powerful its influence on the wine. For this reason, lesser wines are not often aged in wood, as the wine would be overpowered by it. Fine French Burgundies, on the other hand, are aged in small oak barrels, which impart a unique flavor and bouquet to them.

Stainless-steel tanks are the newest and most popular alternative to aging wine in wood. The tanks are temperature-controlled, which permits the winemaker to slowly ferment wine at a low temperature, thus retaining its fruitiness and delicacy while preventing oxidation. Oxidation, also known as maderization, is an undesirable process through which young and fruity white wine becomes stale, flat and brownish in color.

Finally, most wineries today have complex processing plants with automated bottling systems. The basic principle of bottle-aging—or aging wine in bottles after first aging it in barrels or tanks—is less time for dry and more time for sweet wines.

What Are the Three Basic Types of Wine?

Table Wine

Any wine that is still, not sparkling, and has not been "fortified" by the addition of brandy. Table wines contain 8 to 14 percent alcohol.

Sparkling Wine

Sparkling wine contains bubbles of carbon dioxide gas, which are produced naturally in the fermentation process or added to the wine. The most famous sparkling wine is Champagne. Sparkling wines also contain 8 to 14 percent alcohol.

Fortified Wine

Fortified wine is wine to which brandy has been added to "fortify" it, or make it stronger and more alcoholic. The most famous fortified wines are Madeira, Port and Sherry. Fortified wines contain 17 to 22 percent alcohol. (Fortified wine won't be covered in this book.)

What Are the Important Factors in Winemaking?

Although wine is made throughout the world, wines are as variable as the cultures in which they are produced. Some regions of the world, such as the Napa and Sonoma valleys in California and Bordeaux and Burgundy in France, have conditions that are naturally harmonious to the making of fine wines.

Five Factors Determine the Quality of a Wine

There are five basic components that determine the quality of every wine. These are where the wine is made; the type of soil in which the grapes are grown; the climate; the varieties of grapes that are used; and the individual style of the winemaker.

Where Wine Is Made

Grapes require a hospitable environment in which to grow. They need sun, rain, a certain number of days in which to reach maturity (a growing season) and the proper temperature.

The Soil

The type of soil grapes are grown in affects how those grapes will taste when they are made into wine. The dry and flinty quality of Chablis, for example, is directly attributed to the unique soil in which its grapes are grown.

The Climate

White wines are usually made in northern regions, with shorter growing seasons. Red wines are made in southern regions, because red grapes require longer growing seasons.

The Types of Grapes Used

There are three major categories of grapes: *Vitis vinifera, Vitis labrusca* and hybrids of the two preceding types.

• The finest wines are made from *Vitis vinifera,* which are native to Europe but now grown in countries all around the world.

• *Vitis labrusca* are grapes native to the United States and are more likely these days to wind up in jams and jellies than in wine.

• Many winemakers in the eastern United States, where the weather is not as felicitous as in California, use hybrids; these combine the sturdiness of labrusca with the delicacy of vinifera.

Who Makes the Wine

Winemakers are the ultimate arbiters of the style of their wines. They determine what vines to grow, when to harvest the grapes, how to blend them, whether to age wines and if so for how long, whether to ferment wine in oak barrels or stainless steel vats and every other issue that comes up along the way. And winemakers are also, of course, subject to the vagaries of the weather.

WINEMAKERS AND LOCATION

A common aphorism in real estate is that the three most important considerations are location, location and location. Location is also one of the key variables in winemaking. In fact Rhône winemaker Paul Jaboulet has named both his red and white wines "Parallele '45.'" His vineyard is located on the 45th latitude—exactly in the middle of the equator and the north pole.

Does the Color of the Grape Determine the Color of the Wine?

Not necessarily. Blanc de Blancs is a white wine made from white grapes, while Blanc de Noirs is a white wine made from red grapes. Blush wines such as white Zinfandel are pale rosés made from red grapes.

Should All Wines Be Aged?

No. The vast majority of wines fall into the simple category and are meant for casual drinking within a year of their production.

Only about 10 percent of the world's wines are complex and benefit from aging. Complex red wines rich in tannins will taste bitter if drunk too young. And complex white wines such as French Burgundy or Sauternes gain in depth and flavor as they age.

What Are Wine Vintages?

A vintage is the year in which the grapes used to make a wine were harvested. The date is useful for you to know about all types of wine; simple wines are meant to be drunk young, while complex wines require time to mature.

Some vintages are considered better than others. Vintages are extremely important in regions such as Bordeaux and Burgundy in France, where erratic weather makes the wines of certain years appreciably better or worse than others. Wine critics rate these years on vintage charts.

Vintage Champagne is different from vintage still wines. Vintages are declared only when a Champagne is made from the grapes of a particularly excellent year, and not all wine-makers declare vintages in the same year. Vintage years appear on the label of vintage Champagnes, which must be made 100 percent from a particular vintage. They are more expensive than nonvintage Champagnes, and less representative of the typical house style.

What Is Acidity in Wine?

White wines generally have more acidity than reds. While all wines contain natural acids, the amount is important: too little acid makes a wine bland, while too much makes it taste vinegary. The right amount of acid, in balance with a wine's other components, makes it taste crisp, clean and lively.

What Are Tannins in Wine?

Tannins are substances naturally found in the skins, stalks and pips of grapes. They can also occur when wine is aged in oak barrels. Red wines generally have more tannins than whites; tannins, like acidity, impart dryness and permit aging. If complex red wines containing tannins are drunk too young, they may taste harsh.

Types of Wine Grapes

There are a number of grape names that you are likely to encounter again and again on wine labels. These grapes will also be mentioned in later chapters, as the United States and other countries around the globe use them to make wine. Following is an introduction to some of the world's most important wine grapes.

Barbera

• An Italian grape used in making wines of that name in Italy's renowned Piedmont region.
• Barbera wines share the earthy flavor of wines made from the Nebbiolo grape, but are not as powerful or robust.
• In California rich and full-bodied wines are made from this grape.

Cabernet Franc

• A softer grape than the Cabernet Sauvignon, with which it is often blended. American Cabernet Sauvignons from California to Long Island often contain some proportion of this grape.
• Bourgueil and Chinon, fruity wines with hints of berries and herbs, are made from Cabernet Franc in France's Loire Valley.

Cabernet Sauvignon

• The noble wine grape of French red Bordeaux and some of the finest red wines in the United States.
• Wines that are made from 100 percent Cabernet Sauvignon are hard, tannic and durable; in fact they should be aged

for at least five years in order to soften and reach their true potential. This was the original style of American Cabernet Sauvignons. Now, like Bordeaux winemakers, Americans are beginning to blend Cabernet Sauvignon with grapes such as Cabernet Franc or Merlot, in order to add softness and complexity to the wine.

• Cabernet Sauvignons are produced by other countries around the world, such as Argentina, Australia, Chile, Hungary and Italy.

Chardonnay

• In France, Chardonnay is used to make all the best dry white Burgundies, such as Chablis and Chassagne-Montrachet. French wines made from the Chardonnay grape are more acidic than American Chardonnays.

• American Chardonnays tend to be full-bodied, intense, alcoholic and fruity. Their rich and buttery flavor is often accompanied by a complex oakiness due to aging in oak casks.

• Chardonnays are produced by other countries around the world, including Argentina, Australia, Chile and Spain.

• Chardonnay is combined with Pinot Noir to make the world's finest sparkling wines, including Champagne.

Chenin Blanc

• The Chenin Blanc grape is one of the most widely planted varieties in the Loire Valley in France.

• In France, Chenin Blanc is used to make Vouvray, a white wine which ranges from dry to semi-sweet to sweet.

• In California, wines made from the Chenin Blanc grape are either very dry or semi-sweet. California Chenin Blanc is a simple aperitif wine.

Gamay, Napa Gamay and Gamay Beaujolais

• The Gamay grape is used in France to make Beaujolais, a simple, fresh, fruity, young red wine.

• France also makes Beaujolais Nouveau from Gamay.

• Italy uses Gamay and other grapes to make Vino novello, their answer to France's Beaujolais Nouveau.

• In California, Gamay may be called Napa Gamay or Gamay Beaujolais, and is used to make the same style wines as the light and fruity Beaujolais of France.

Garnacha

• A red Spanish grape related to the French Grenache of the Rhône Valley.
• It is blended with Tempranillo to make Spanish Riojas.

Gewürztraminer

• Gewürz is the German word for spice, and the white wines made from this grape are distinctively spicy. They are made in Germany, Austria, the Alsace region of France and California.

Grenache

• The grape used to make Tavel rosés in France, and blended with Syrah in the Rhône Valley to make Châteauneuf-du-Pape.
• Also used to make rosé wines in California. One of the most popular California rosés is the Grenache rosé, a light and perfumey wine, on the sweet side, made by Almaden.

Melon

• Used to make crisp and light dry white Muscadets in France's Loire Valley.

Merlot

• A soft, round and plummy red grape. Less tannic than Cabernet Sauvignon, with which it is often blended.
• Used to make some French red Bordeaux, such as Château Pétrus.
• The United States, Chile and Italy are among the countries that make Merlot wine.

Müller-Thurgau

• A grape that is a cross between Riesling and Sylvaner.
• Used to make austere white wines in Germany and Italy.
• Young Müller-Thurgaus will taste harsh; they need a year or two of aging in order to soften.

Nebbiolo

• Ruby-red, powerful, robust and full-bodied. Considered by many wine critics to be the best wine grape of Italy.
• The grape of wines such as Barolo, Gattinara and Barbaresco in Italy's famous Piedmont region.
• Noted for their huge violet-scented bouquet.
• Wines made from the Nebbiolo grape benefit from aging.

Petite Sirah

• A variety of California grape originally thought to be the Syrah grape of France's Rhône Valley.
• Can produce dark, full-textured wines reminiscent of those of the Rhône.

Pinot Blanc

• Makes a simple dry white wine, characteristically round and soft. A popular wine of the Alsace region in France.

Pinot Noir

• The grape used to make the great red Burgundy of France.
• Also thrives in Oregon and the cooler climates of growing regions in northern California, such as Napa, Sonoma and Mendocino.
• Makes red wines that are softer, fruitier and less tannic (or dry) than Cabernet Sauvignon.
• One of the wine grapes being made into a popular new California category, vin gris. Vin gris is a pale dry rosé or blush wine made from red grapes.

• Combined with Chardonnay to make the world's finest sparkling wines, including Champagne.

Riesling

• Also referred to as Johannisberg Riesling, the best German wine grape.
• Produces aromatic white wine, lightweight, low in alcohol, with a flowery bouquet. Dry or off-dry in taste.
• Ready to drink when a year or two old, although it can last well longer.
• Rieslings are made by other countries, including the United States, France (the Alsace region), Austria and Chile.

Sangiovese

• The famous Chianti from Tuscany is made from this native Italian grape.
• Chiantis are sturdy and full-bodied, and less tannic (or dry) than wines made from the Nebbiolo grape.

Sauvignon Blanc

• Used to make a simple white wine, crisp and acidic. May be described as oaky, fruity, herbaceous, grassy or lemony.
• Meant to be drunk on the young side, when a year or two old.

SAUVIGNON BLANC OR FUMÉ BLANC?

Legend has it that Robert Mondavi couldn't sell his Sauvignon Blanc as Sauvignon Blanc, so he simply renamed it Fumé Blanc. Suddenly Fumé Blanc was all the rage, everyone bought it, and other winemakers followed Mondavi's clever marketing strategy.

• A popular American wine, which also goes by the name
of Fumé Blanc.
• Australia and Chile also produce Sauvignon Blancs.
• In France, the dry white wines Pouilly-Fumé and Sancerre
are made with 100 percent Sauvignon Blanc. The soil of the
Loire Valley combines with the Sauvignon Blanc grape to impart distinctive bouquets to these wines.

Sémillon

• Rich, ripe and fruity. Alone it is somewhat aromatic.
• Often blended with Chardonnay or Sauvignon grapes,
which balance the aromatic nature of Sémillon with their rel-
ative crispness and acidity.
• In the white Bordeaux wines of France, Sémillon is com-
bined in varying ratios with Sauvignon Blanc to produce dry
Graves wines or sweet Sauternes.
• A popular grape in American and Australian wines.

Shiraz

• The strongest, brawniest Australian red. Can be smoky or
spicy.
• The Australian equivalent of the Syrah grape used in the
Rhône wines of France.
• Often combined with Cabernet Sauvignon, resulting in
rich, complex and full-bodied wines.

Sylvaner

• A light white grape made into simple inexpensive wines
in France and Germany.

Syrah

• The noble red grape of France's Rhône Valley.
• Produces intense wines with heavy berry or pepper
flavors.
• Some California vintners, such as Joseph Phelps, make
sturdy Rhône-style reds using the Syrah grape.

Tempranillo

• A grape native to Spain, blended with Garnacha to make red Riojas.

Zinfandel

• Zinfandel is usually considered a native American grape, since no one has successfully been able to trace its history back to Europe.

• Zinfandel is less complex than Cabernet Sauvignon and Pinot Noir, and more intense and alcoholic.

• Some Zinfandels are smooth and elegant; others are full-bodied, powerful and rough-edged. Read the back of the label to see which variety the winemaker has chosen to create.

TWO

How to Choose the Right Wine

A basic premise in choosing a wine is to secure good value for your money—and wine is a good value whenever you find the right bottle for the right occasion at the right price.

Most importantly, the wine you *enjoy* is the right wine for you. Forget about that old rule of white wine with white meats and red wine with reds. Lighter wines, whether white or red, go well with lighter foods, or you can drink them on their own; heavier or full-bodied wines—white or red—better complement heavier or richer foods.

And at most wine stores and restaurants you can count on the merchant or waiter to help you out with your choice, suggesting a variety of wines at prices you can afford. The message: you don't have to be a wine expert or a millionaire to enjoy a glass of wine.

Shopping for Wine

It's a good idea to shop around for a store you really like, and then regularly patronize it. Get to know one merchant or salesperson in the store. Once your regular salesperson gets to know you and the type of wine you like, he or she can make useful new suggestions that can broaden your wine horizons.

It also helps to become familiar with the various types of wine—how they taste, what they cost, when you might best

17

like to drink them, with or without food—in order to choose
the bottle of wine that is right for you. This book will help
you do that. Following are a few tips to keep in mind, though,
that will make your trip to the wine store a pleasurable one.

• Don't be afraid to ask questions. Most wine merchants
enjoy the discussion and can make helpful suggestions.

• Take your time and wander through the store. Wine is an
investment that rewards consideration.

• In most stores, wines are organized according to the country in which the wines were made.

• Think about the occasion you are buying wine for. How
many people do you intend to serve? What food are you serving with the wine?

• Larger stores often buy wine in greater bulk and are then
able to sell it at more competitive prices. But smaller stores
may offer more personalized services.

• Prices vary widely. If you see that the markup on a wine
is considerably higher than you think it should be, chances are
you'll be able to find a better price at another store. Do some
comparison shopping until you find prices you're comfortable
with.

• If you come across a wine that is significantly lower-
priced than you think it should be—stop! Don't automatically
buy it. Read the label to make sure the wine you're buying is
the real thing. As you will see, labels can be confusing. But
if you have indeed spotted a bargain, snap it up and enjoy.

Unraveling the Mystery of Basic Wine Terminology

In order to effectively communicate with a wine merchant or
waiter, it's useful to be familiar with some of the terms com-

monly used to describe wine. (A more complete list is available in the Glossary.)

• *Acidity* is an important part of what makes a wine taste good. White wines are generally more acidic than reds. Too little acidity makes a wine bland, while too much makes it taste vinegary. More adjectives experts use to describe a wine with a proper acid balance: fresh, lively, tangy, and zesty.

• *Dry* is a term used to describe wines in which the sugar has fermented into alcohol, and is contrasted to *sweet*. If the wine is extremely dry, experts refer to it as *bone-dry*. Dry wines may also be referred to as tasting *crisp* and *clean*.

• The *alcoholic content* of wine may vary from 8 to 14 percent, with most wines falling somewhere around 12 percent. Alcohol, one of the principal components of wine, is a product of the fermentation of the grapes. Alcohol contributes to the taste of wine and also acts as a preservative. The alcoholic content of wine and the rate at which it is consumed contribute to wine's inebriating effect.

• *Tannins* are substances found naturally in the skins, stalks and pips of grapes; they also appear when wine is aged in wood barrels. Tannins impart dryness to a wine and act as a preservative. They are more common in red than white wines.

• In white wines, skins are separated from the grapes at the outset of production. In red wines, skins and juice are allowed to ferment together until further alcohol is produced.

• A wine with *longevity* is one that will age well. Acidity, alcoholic content and tannins all contribute to the longevity of a wine. The initial ingredients and the care with which they are made increase the value of fine wines over time. But not all wines improve with age. In fact, ninety percent of wines made today should be consumed within a year of their production.

• The *body* of a wine consists of its weight and alcoholic content. Both red and white wines range from light-bodied to medium-bodied to full-bodied. Extremely full-bodied reds are often referred to as *robust*.

• *Full-bodied* red wines are high in alcohol and soluble solids from the grape, called *extract* or *sediment*. They generally need time to age, or mature, and taste weighty and substantial. Other adjectives wine connoisseurs, or oenophiles, might use to describe full reds: *rich, robust, powerful, deep-flavored, deeply colored* and *velvety*.

• *Fruity* wines have the fresh, springlike flavor and perfume of ripe grapes. Fruity wines are generally drunk when they are young, as their characteristics fade with age.

• *Sweet* wines have a high sugar content. They may taste sweet either because sugar was added to them or because they were made from overripe grapes.

• A *well-balanced* wine is one with a harmonious agreement among its various components—acidity, fruitiness, sweetness, tannins and alcohol content.

General Hints on How to Read a Wine Label

A wide array of wines of different styles from different countries stand on the wine shelves of your local store. Here are a few hints on how to sort them out.

Look for the Most Specific Information

In general, the more specific the label, the better the wine. For example, if the region in which the wine was made is mentioned, it is usually a finer wine; if the vineyard in the region is mentioned, even better.

Governments Play a Major Role

Each government's regulation of its wine production is critical in determining the consistent quality of the country's wines. A wine must meet certain minimum requirements in order to receive a state seal of approval on the label.

The Back Label

And don't neglect to read the label on the back of the bottle—it often includes a more detailed description of the wine, including additional information about who made it, how it was made and helpful hints about how it might best be served.

How to Read an American Wine Label

The American wine industry is regulated by the Bureau of Alcohol, Tobacco, and Firearms (BATF), and increasing production and consumption of wine in the United States has prompted stricter regulation. In 1983 the BATF defined a *varietal* wine as one that contains at least 75 percent of the grape for which it is named.

American wines today, then, can be seen as falling into two basic categories: jug wines and varietals.

Jug Wines

Jug wines are simple, uncomplicated wines. So-called because they were originally bottled in jugs, today they come in all shapes and sizes and may include the name of French wine regions on their labels, such as American Chablis or Hearty Burgundy.

American jug wine is in fact the equivalent of French *vin ordinaire*. In France *vin ordinaire* can be served from the tap, much as beer is served in the United States.

Jug wines are the perfect answer when you are entertaining a large group of people. While an average-sized bottle of wine is 750 milliliters and holds six glasses of wine, jugs may range from 1.5 liters to 4 liters—or twelve to thirty-two glasses.

Large bottles of jug wines are available in all the major stores, most retailing for under ten dollars. Although their popularity has slipped in recent years as consumers explore the new dimensions of varietal wines, jug wines still account for 48 percent of American wine sales.

Varietal Wines

Varietal wines are of higher quality than jug wines. They are labeled according to the individual grape from which the wine is primarily made, such as Cabernet Sauvignon, Chardonnay, Pinot Noir or Zinfandel. As noted, by U.S. law varietal wines must contain at least 75 percent of the grape named on the label.

California led the United States in making fine varietals. Naming wines after grapes rather than geographical areas was a way to distinguish these more complex varietal wines from simple, everyday jug wines, which, as mentioned above, often have French place-names such as Chablis or Burgundy on their labels.

As more consumers grow familiar with the most famous wine regions of the United States, such as the Napa and Sonoma valleys in California, this information is taking a more prominent place on the label and in advertising. This is likewise true of American vineyards and winemakers.

How to Read an Australian Wine Label

Australian wine labels generally follow the American format: the name of the grape from which they are primarily made takes prominence on the label over their place of origin. The best Australian wines carry varietal names of grapes such as Shiraz, Cabernet Sauvignon, Chardonnay, Sémillon and Johannisberg Riesling.

LABELS CAN BE CONFUSING

When you're purchasing a bottle of wine, it is useful to be aware of the ins and outs of reading a label. For example, there is Chablis from France, a dry white wine produced from a mere 2,600-acre patch of French soil. This is a very fine wine priced in the twenty-to-thirty-dollar range.

Then there are bottles labeled "American Chablis," usually jug wines priced under ten dollars. These wines are usually simple, uncomplicated, fresh and drinkable—but should not be confused with French Chablis, which is a complex dry white wine.

How to Read a Chilean Wine Label

South American wines are good bargains, and Chile's wine industry is one of the best-regulated in the world. Chilean wine labels include the name of the grape, the producer of the wine and the region where the wine was made.

How to Read a French Wine Label

The Appellation d'Origine Contrôlée (AOC) is the branch of the French government that regulates the wine industry and sets minimum standards for the fine wines of France. These fine wines constitute 15 percent of all French wine; the other 85 percent is *vin ordinaire,* or "ordinary wine."

With the exception of Alsace, which labels its wines according to grape variety, French wines are named after the region in which they are made. France is widely considered by wine experts to produce some of the best wines in the world.

How to Read a German Wine Label

German wine labels have typically been among the most difficult to understand, although attempts have been made in recent years to simplify them.

German wines are strictly regulated by the German Ministry
of Agriculture. Look for the region in which the wine was
made, the grape name and the vintage. Better wines also carry
the name of the vineyard, but may or may not include the
name of the grape.

How to Read an Italian Wine Label

The words *Denominazione di Origine Controllata* appear on
Italian wine labels. These words on the label mean that the
wine was made in accordance with strict government regulations and conforms to at least minimum standards of quality.

How to Read a Spanish Wine Label

Spanish wines are considered "one of the best-kept secrets of
the wine world," according to wine expert Frank Prial of *The
New York Times.*

Labels follow the French method, with the source of grapes
narrowed to certain areas or "estates." This precise method
of labeling produces a highly consistent style of wine. Information on the labels may include the producer of the wine,
the region where the wine was made and the vineyard.

Some Basic Categories of Wine

While experts agree that every bottle of wine is different,
wines naturally fall into certain categories. Although there is
considerable overlapping in these categories—one person's
full-bodied might be another's robust—distinctions are made

according to such criteria as the type of grape used to make the wine, the soil in which the grape was grown, the climate, when the grapes were harvested, to what extent and how the wine was aged and the style of the individual winemaker.

All these factors combine to determine the quality of a wine. But keep in mind that every categorization of wines is somewhat arbitrary; one can be as simplistic as red, white and rosé, or as complicated as a division into categories such as the sixty-one properties making up the 1855 classification of Bordeaux, or the twenty-three hundred or so Italian wine labels. Following are some helpful guidelines, including basic categories of wine, accompanied by an elaboration on each one.

- Simple Dry White Wines:
  Light-bodied, crisp, acidic. Easy to drink. Young, fresh and inexpensive. Serve chilled, alone or with food.

- Complex Dry White Wines:
  Full-bodied, dry and more expensive. Grow in depth and complexity with age. May taste oaky or fruity. Avoid overchilling, and serve with food.

- Aromatic White Wines:
  Lightweight, low in alcohol, with a flowery bouquet. Usually inexpensive. Can be sweet or dry. Serve chilled, alone or with food.

- Sweet White Wines:
  Sweet, and the best ones are usually expensive. Serve them slightly chilled, as an aperitif before a meal, or after a meal, alone or with a dessert.

- Sparkling Wines:
  Wine with bubbles. Usually white, but may be rosé; ranges from dry (brut) to sweet (demi-sec). The "Champagne Method" (méthode champenoise) is labor-intensive and expensive; consequently sparkling wines made in this method are also expensive. But, as in most categories, bargains can be found. Serve chilled, alone or with food.

- Rosé Wines, Blush Wines and Vin Gris:
  Young, fresh and usually inexpensive. Range from sweet to dry. Serve chilled, alone or with light foods.

- Light Red Wines:
  Light- to medium-bodied. Young, fresh, fruity and in-expensive. Serve very light ones chilled, those with more body at room temperature, alone or with food.

- Full Red Wines:
  Strong and tannic, ranging from full-bodied to robust. May taste woody, jammy, peppery or fruity, depending on such factors as the grapes they were made from and how they were aged. More expensive than light reds. Serve at room temperature, with food.

Simple Dry White Wines

Sampling a simple dry white is a perfect way for you to enter the world of wine. These wines are light, tasty and inexpensive. Drink them when they are young.

How to Serve Simple White Wines

Serve light whites well-chilled, either alone or with fish, chicken, salad—or even strongly flavored dishes that would smother the flavor of a more delicate wine.

Crisp, fruity and light white wines are perfect for hot summer days, times when you want something ice-cold to drink. Light wines do not have the pronounced flavor of complex ones, which shouldn't be served as cold.

Sound, Simple and Economical

The carafe of house wine you order in a restaurant is usually a simple dry white. Most jug wines also fit into this category. If you want a white wine spritzer, simply add ice and club soda. Simple, economical and extremely drinkable white wines are made by countries all around the world.

A SELECTION OF SIMPLE DRY WHITE WINES

The following white wines are generally available for under ten dollars. For a more comprehensive listing, consult the Appendix.

- Bald Eagle Sauvignon Blanc (California)
- Fetzer Fumé Blanc (California)
- Groth Sauvignon Blanc (California)
- Robert Mondavi Fumé Blanc (California)
- Los Vascos Sauvignon Blanc (Chile)
- Santiago "1541" Sauvignon Blanc (Chile)
- Beaujolais Blanc (George Duboeuf, France)
- Cler' Blanc (France)
- Entre-Deux-Mers (France)
- St. Véran (France)
- Frascati (Italy)
- Pinot Grigio (Italy)
- Soave (Italy)
- Ruffino Orvieto (Italy)
- Gran Viña Sol (Spain)
- Marqués de Cáceres (Spain)
- Marqués de Riscal (Spain)
- Viña Sol (Spain)

More Complex Dry White Wines

The great white Burgundies of France and the best dry white Chardonnay wines of the United States are good examples of the more complex dry white wines. Most complex whites are expensive.

How Are Complex White Wines Made?

Many wines in this category are made with Chardonnay grapes and, unlike simple whites, are aged in oak barrels before bottling. The resulting wines are full-bodied and mouth-filling.

How to Serve Them

Complex whites are meant to be drunk with food. Avoid overchilling them, as then you will lose their full flavor.

A SELECTION OF COMPLEX DRY WHITE WINES

The following more complex dry white wines are only a sampling of what is available in various price ranges. In the bargain department, the wines are borderline entries in the complex category—some critics might pop them back up with the light whites, or create a nice medium category.

Bargains Under Ten Dollars
- Bald Eagle (California)
- Fetzer "Sundial" Chardonnay (California)
- Mâcon-Lugny "Les Charmes" (France)
- Mâcon-Villages (Georges Duboeuf, France)

If You Want to Splurge: Chardonnays in the Ten-to-Twenty-Dollar Range
- Edna Valley (California)
- Freemark Abbey (California)
- Frog's Leap (California)
- Hargrave (New York)
- Lenz (New York)
- Liberty School (California)
- Robert Mondavi (California)
- Parker (California)
- Paumonok (New York)
- Silverado (California)
- Simi (California)
- Southhampton (New York)

CALIFORNIA CHARDONNAYS

For twenty to thirty dollars, you can own a bottle of Acacia, Cakebread, Grgich Hills, Jordan or Staglin Chardonnay. The owner of Grgich Hills, Mike Grgich, is known as the "Mr. Chardonnay" of California. Shari Staglin, the owner of Staglin Family Vineyards in Napa Valley, provided the Chardonnay for a Capitol Hill luncheon honoring Queen Elizabeth II.

Where Are Complex White Wines Made?

Complex dry white wines, just like simple ones, are produced by countries around the world, including France, the United States, Australia, Austria, Bulgaria, Hungary, Italy, South Africa and Yugoslavia.

Aromatic White Wines

These white wines are lightweight, low in alcohol and have fruity or flowery scents. They should be drunk somewhat chilled. Many aromatic wines can be found for under ten dollars a bottle.

German Aromatics

The German variety of aromatic wine combines crisp fresh fruitiness with an underlying sweetness. Wine labels may say Qualitätswein, Kabinett or Spätlese, and wines are most often made from the Riesling and Gewürztraminer grapes. The brand you're probably most familiar with is the famous Blue Nun Liebfraumilch.

Some people feel that the sweet taste of German aromatics does not mix well with food. If you're among this group, drink your wine before a meal, as an aperitif. Or after a meal, as a digestif.

Other Aromatic Wines Around the World

Many other regions of the world also produce aromatic white wines. *Time* magazine quoted the famous wine critic Robert M. Parker, Jr., as calling the Alsace region of France "the world's most underrated white wine region."

The aromatic white wines of Alsace—spicy Rieslings and Gewürztraminers—are, in contrast to German aromatics, flowery but *dry*. This, according to Mr. Parker, makes them "ideal companions to . . . shellfish, grilled chicken and pasta salad. (Gewürztraminer has a peculiar affinity for Chinese and Indian dishes.)"

California Rieslings and Gewürztraminers are generally more full-bodied than their European counterparts and, like Alsace aromatics, go well with food. Austria, England, Italy, New Zealand and Yugoslavia also produce aromatic white wines.

A TASTE TEST OF AROMATIC WHITE WINE

These wines are something of an acquired taste. Before buying a bottle, you may want to try ordering a glass at a restaurant. If you choose a German aromatic wine, order it before or after your dinner. If you're eating Indian food, have a glass of an Alsace or California Riesling with your dinner.

Sweet White Wines

Sweet white wines, like sweet desserts, come after a meal. They should be served slightly chilled, alone or with dessert. At the start of a meal the sugar in a sweet wine would simply ruin your appetite.

Sweet wines are more of an acquired taste than simpler table wines. Yet at their best they are among the finest wines in the world, extremely rich and full of seductive fruit flavors.

How Are Sweet White Wines Made?

Sweet wines are made in one of two ways: either from sugar added to wine, or from grapes picked late in the season, as their flavor becomes intensely concentrated. This second process is very risky and expensive for winemakers.

The Most Famous Sweet White Wines

The most famous member of this category is the French Sauternes. Other sweet wines include Barsac, also made in the Sauternes region of France.

In addition there are German sweet white wines—very rare, very expensive and very difficult for those of us who do not speak German to pronounce—called Auslesen, Beerenauslesen, Trockenbeerenauslesen and Eiswein.

Australia, Austria, Cyprus, Hungary, Portugal, Sicily, Spain and the United States are among the other countries that produce sweet white wines.

A TASTE TEST OF SWEET WHITE WINE

Sweet white wines are usually expensive and are more of an acquired taste than simpler table wines. Before buying a bottle, order a glass after dinner in a restaurant or accept a glass from your host following a dinner party.

Sparkling Wines

Champagne

The delicious sparkling bubbles of Champagne are probably the most famous in the world. Without Champagne, how could

we get married? Celebrate a birthday, anniversary or gradua-
tion? Launch a ship?

As the French are first to note, the only real Champagne—
Champagne with a capital *C*—comes from the sixty-thousand-
acre Champagne region of France. Most French Champagnes
start in the twenty-to-thirty-dollar range.

Other Sparkling Wines of the World

While today we continue to savor the Champagnes of
Champagne, almost all other wine regions of the world produce their own versions of sparkling wine. Many are considerably less expensive than Champagne. Germany makes
sparkling wines called Sekt, while Italy offers a sweeter ver-
sion of sparkling wine, called Asti Spumante. Other regions
of France make sparkling wine called Crémants.

The Sparkling Wines of the United States

In California domestic vineyards such as Schramsberg and
Korbel work side by side with the American vineyards of Taittinger and Moët & Chandon. There, as in France, Chardonnay
and Pinot Noir grapes are combined to make the finest sparkling wines.

The Champagne Method

The labels of many sparkling wines that do not say "Champagne" will often indicate that the wine was made in the
"méthode champenoise," or in the same style as Champagne.

In the champagne method yeast and sugar are added to a
bottle of still wine, and secondary fermentation takes place in
the bottle. The yeast converts the sugar into alcohol and, as
the process takes place, carbon dioxide is released. Trapped
in the corked and wired bottle, it forms bubbles.

Champagne Punch

The Gallo Winery of California makes what is probably the
most economical champagne in the world—André, at less than

five dollars a bottle. André is a wonderful choice when you want to stretch your dollars and yet remain festive. It's great to use in champagne punch or to make that wonderful brunch concoction of sparkling wine and orange juice, Mimosa.

A SELECTION OF SPARKLING WINES

The following sparkling wines are only a sampling of what is available in various price ranges. For a more comprehensive listing, consult the Appendix.

Bargains: Sparkling Wines for Under Ten Dollars
- Asti Spumante (Italy)
- Boyer Brut (France)
- Codorníu (Spain)
- Crémant d'Alsace Brut (France)
- Freixenet (Spain)
- Henkell (Germany)

If You Want to Splurge: Sparkling Wines in the Ten-to-Twenty-Dollar Range
- Chandon Napa Brut (California)
- Korbel Natural (California)
- Mumm's Cuvée Napa (California)
- Taittinger's Domaine Carneros Brut (California)

For the Most Special Occasions: The Twenty-to-Thirty-Dollar Range
- Iron Horse Brut (California)
- Jordan Sparkling Wine (California)
- Moët & Chandon (France)
- Perrier-Jouet (France)
- Taittinger (France)
- Veuve Clicquot (France)

Sparkling Wine Terminology

A final note about sparkling wine: the terminology on the labels may be somewhat confusing. An "extra dry" or "demi-sec" Champagne is actually gentle and fruity; it is the "brut" Champagne that is dry.

Rosé Wines, Blush Wines and Vin Gris

Like simple dry white wines, rosés, also referred to as blush wines and vin gris, are a perfect way to enter the world of wine. Rosés vary in taste from sweet to dry; many sell for under ten dollars. Rosés are meant to be drunk when they are young and fresh. Serve them chilled, alone or with light foods.

A New Trend in Rosé Wines

Rosé wines are experiencing a new surge of popularity in the United States. White Zinfandel—a popular pale pink, or blush, wine made when the red skins of the Zinfandel grape are removed—is crisp, light and easy to drink. Another new

---

A SELECTION OF ROSÉ WINES

The following rosé wines are generally available for under ten dollars. For a more comprehensive listing, consult the Appendix.

- Almaden Gamay Rosé (California)
- Almaden Grenache Rosé (California)
- Gallo Pink Chablis (California)
- Gallo Red Rosé (California)
- Simi Cabernet Rosé (California)

California category is vin gris, a pale dry rosé or blush wine made from red grapes.

Famous French Rosés

The most renowned rosé wine in the world may be the bone dry French Tavel; this is a more expensive wine, retailing in the fifteen-to-twenty-dollar range. And then there's the ultimate luxury, the Rolls Royce of all rosés—pink Champagne! These glamorous, glorious, dramatic and delicious wines are priced accordingly, from thirty to one hundred dollars a bottle.

Light Red Wines

Sampling light red wines is another good way to enter the world of wine. Light-bodied reds range from the smooth blends of grapes we find in jug wines, to the fruity and well-balanced Beaujolais. Many are priced under ten dollars.

How to Serve Light Red Wines

Treat light reds in the same way you do simple whites—drink them when they are young. Serve them chilled, on their own or with food. You'll find them lively and refreshing.

Simple, Sound and Economical

House wines in restaurants are usually light reds. And a red wine can easily be dressed up for a party—simply take a bottle of red jug wine, add some ice cubes, club soda and fruit, and invite your friends over for a Sangria fiesta.

Where Are Light Red Wines Made?

Light red wines are made by countries around the world. But the most famous wine in this category is probably the French Beaujolais, one of the freshest and fruitiest young red wines in the world. Georges Duboeuf is known as the King of Beaujolais, and it is always safe to buy a bottle of Beaujolais with his name on it.

Beaujolais Nouveau is a very young species of Beaujolais—in fact only weeks old when it reaches the United States each November. This quaffable red bargain, at only five dollars or so per bottle, represents an exceptional buy.

Italy is now making a similar wine, called Vino Novello. These very young wines are also meant to be drunk very young, preferably within six months after they are made. And Italy, in addition to Vino Novello, offers popular favorites such as Ruffino Chianti, Valpolicella and Bardolino.

Another well-liked, fruity and well-balanced light red is Sangre de Toro (that is, "Blood of the Bull") of Spain. A little plastic bull is looped around the neck of each bottle.

California's answer to Beaujolais is Zinfandel. But here caution should be exercised. There are two types of Zinfandel:

THE VARIETIES OF BEAUJOLAIS

The best Beaujolais is not necessarily labeled Beaujolais. It is called Cru Beajolais. *Cru* means growth, and in the case of Beaujolais refers to designated villages or communes that produce the region's highest quality wines. They are usually priced under fifteen dollars and come from one of the following villages in the Beaujolais area of France:

- Brouilly
- Chénas
- Chiroubles
- Côte de Brouilly
- Fleurie
- Juliénas
- Morgon
- Moulin-à-Vent
- Saint-Amour

one is the light and fruity cousin of Beaujolais, while the other
is a heavier and richer wine, similar to a Cabernet Sauvignon.
California's Zinfandels tend to be a little pricier than imports,
in the ten-to-twenty-dollar range.

Full Red Wines

Full or full-bodied red wines are considered by wine critics to
be the most important of all wines. They are the backbone of
any serious collector's wine cellar. The balance of acidity, alcoholic content and tannins gives these wines a strong, dry
quality.

Time to Mature

Most critics agree that full reds need time for maturing. In
vineyards they are first aged in barrels or steel vats, and then
bottles. Most need to be aged at least five years before they
begin to reach their fullest and richest potential. This is re-
flected in their price; you are more likely to find bargains in
younger full red wines.

When to Serve Full-Bodied Red Wine

What do you serve full red wines with? They are an excellent accompaniment to roast chicken and cheese, as well as
lamb and beef. As with all wines, experiment with them yourself and see what best fits your own taste.

The Full Red Wines of France

Full red wines are produced all around the globe. The red
Bordeaux, Burgundy and Rhône wines of France are among
the most rich and elegant wines in the world. Many Bordeaux
and Burgundies are unfortunately out of the reach of average
consumers; most don't even squeeze into the twenty-to-thirty-
dollar category. However, fine Rhône wines are often still
available at bargain prices.

A SELECTION OF FULL RED WINES

The prices of full red wines are as variable as their places of origin. The following full red wines are a sampling of what is available in various price ranges. Remember that bargains will usually be found more easily among younger full-bodied reds. And for a more comprehensive listing, consult the Appendix.

Bargains: Full Red Wines for Under Ten Dollars
- Alexander Valley Cabernet Sauvignon (California)
- Chianti Classico (Ruffino, Italy)
- Côtes-du-Rhône (Vidal Fleury, France)
- Los Vascos Cabernet Sauvignon (Chile)
- Rosemount Shiraz Hunter Valley (Australia)

If You Want to Splurge: Full Red Wines in the Ten-to-Twenty-Dollar Range
- Châteauneuf-du-Pape (Guigal, France)
- Pinot Noir (Acacia, California)
- Pinot Noir (Robert Mondavi, California)
- Pinot Noir (Panther Creek, Oregon)

For the Most Special Occasions: The Twenty-to-Thirty-Dollar Range
- Barolo (Renato Ratti, Italy)
- Carmenet Estate Red (California)
- Clos du Bois "Marlstone" (California)
- Nuits St. Georges (Alain Michelot, France)

More Full Red Wines Around the World

To explore full red wines beyond France, you may want to taste the Barolos and Chianti Classicos of Italy; these are deep red, full-bodied and velvety wines.

California's Cabernet Sauvignons, Classic Cuvées and Pinot Noirs rank among the greatest of all red wines. Other states, such as Oregon and New York, also produce highly desirable red wines.

Shiraz grapes in Australia are made into deep-flavored, robust red wines, and countries including Argentina, Chile and New Zealand are producing increasingly powerful and complex Cabernet Sauvignons.

Three

Ordering and Tasting Wines: What You Always Wanted to Know

Many people find it pleasant to taste wine in the company of family and friends. Whether in the restaurant or at home, sampling a variety of wines in a relaxed social environment is an excellent way to explore the world of wine.

Ordering Wine in a Restaurant

Many variables must be considered in choosing a wine in a restaurant: your operating budget, how much wine you wish to order, the styles of wine preferred by you and your companions and which wine or wines will best complement the food you are going to eat.

It is a little bit trickier to choose wine in a restaurant than it is in a store, because you have less time to linger on your consideration when you are seated with your companions in a restaurant. But when you decide to purchase and store wine in your home, the wines you have come to like in these tasting experiments—your tried-and-true favorites—are frequently the best starting point.

The Cost of Wine in Restaurants

In the restaurant as well as in the store, wine is a good value when you find the right bottle at the right price for the right occasion. In fact, price is an even more critical consideration in restaurants, where bottles are more expensive than in stores.

Supply and Demand

Wines in restaurants are usually at least twice the price that they are in wine stores. In addition, the arbitrary laws of supply and demand may sometimes push the price of a California Cabernet Sauvignon sky-high, while ignoring the merits of a good Cabernet Sauvignon from Chile.

Prices Vary According to the Category of Wine

Returning to the basic categories of wine described in Chapter One, simple wines are less expensive than complex ones and, unless you want to splurge for a special occasion, are fine for most meals. Since prices in restaurants are at least double those in wine stores, this would put you in the ten-to-twenty-dollar range.

Sparkling and rosé wines are good choices when your party has ordered a variety of different dishes, since they can complement more foods. Because of their price, however, most people reserve ordering sparkling wine for special occasions.

If you don't know much about wine, you may be tempted to play it safe and simply select a wine in the medium price range. But this is not always the best alternative.

The House Wine

In cost-conscious times, the house carafe may well be the best value for your money. A diner's first impression of a restaurant is often received through the quality of its house wine; many restaurant owners, knowing this, choose sound and economical wines to fill their carafes.

Sometimes the waiter can tell you about the house wine—for example, its style, the grape it was made from, where it was made and by whom—and this is a good sign. But often the only information you will receive is that the restaurant offers a house red, white and rosé.

In any case, it is always a smart move to taste a glass of the house wine before ordering a carafe of it. Then you have the knowledge to choose a carafe of the house wine or to move on to the wine list.

Reading the Wine List

The wine list often arrives with the menus. In case it doesn't, ask your waiter to please bring it to you right away, so you can leisurely peruse the list. Following are a few pointers on wine lists.

• The length of a wine list is not necessarily a measure of its excellence. A small list may still include a range of wine at reasonable prices.

• A good wine list should follow a logical format. For example, wines should be organized according to their style or country of origin.

• Detailed information should be included about each wine, such as its vintage, producer and shipper.

An Opportunity to Explore New Wines

Restaurants afford you an excellent opportunity to sample new wines. Especially when they are available by the glass, a restaurant is the ideal place to experiment with tasting different wines.

Although wines by the glass are relatively more expensive than the same wines by the bottle, it is still more economical to experiment by tasting a single glass of wine in a restaurant than by buying an entire bottle of that wine—which, after all, you may not care for—in a wine store.

Should Expensive Wine Be Ordered in a Restaurant?

The ultimate answer to this question is that it depends on your personal inclination and the size of your wallet. But, as always, there are certain guidelines that can aid you in making a decision.

In restaurants you know well or in very fine restaurants, an expensive wine may be an appropriate choice. But many wine experts feel that the vast majority of medium-quality restaurants are not ideal for expensive complex wines.

Some red wines, for example, benefit from time to "breathe" before they are served. Sediment also needs time to settle to the bottom of the bottle, lest you find remnants of it floating about in your glass.

And last but not least, these wines are already expensive in the wine store and will cost you at least double that price in a restaurant. A better alternative is often to order the house carafe or another economical but tasty choice—and apply your savings to a better bottle you can savor at your leisure in your home.

Selecting a Wine

While you shouldn't allow a waiter to pressure you into making a decision too quickly, once the group has selected what they would like to eat, it is time to choose the wine or wines you would like with your meal.

How much wine to order in a restaurant depends on how many people will be drinking it, how much you want to spend, the type of meal you are having and the individual preferences of you and your companions.

On average, count on each person drinking about four glasses of wine:

- One glass before dinner:
    As an aperitif, or stimulant to the appetite. Sparkling wines are a good choice.

- Two glasses with dinner:
    Here the style of wine or wines depends upon what best complements the meal. Lighter meals call for lighter wines; heavier dishes are best complemented by heavier, more full-bodied wines. Consult Chapter Seven, "Food and Wine," for some specific suggestions.

- One glass after dinner:
    Alone or with dessert. Usually a sweeter wine, such as a French Sauternes, or a late harvest wine from Germany, Alsace or California.

An average-sized bottle of wine contains 750 milliliters, or 25.4 ounces, and holds six glasses. Carafes hold about the same amount, while half bottles and half carafes hold about three glasses. Many restaurants also offer a selection of wines by the glass.

SEDIMENT IN RED WINE

If you order a complex red wine, there is likely to be sediment in the bottom; sediment is natural and desirable in this type of wine, but it will mean that the amount of drinkable wine is slightly reduced.

Dinner for Two

If the meal is a leisurely one, with appetizer, salad, entrée and dessert, two people often share a full bottle of wine. If two people choose entrées that call for different types of wine, order by the glass, half bottle or half carafe. The amount of wine also depends, of course, on individual inclination and the budget you have allotted to the meal.

A quicker and less leisurely meal will require less wine. If it is lunch rather than dinner, many people have a busy schedule to follow and might choose to have just one or two glasses of wine. In this case order by the glass or half bottle.

A Dinner Party

What if the group dining with you orders dishes that call for different types of wine? In another era this problem was neatly circumvented: the host simply ordered for the whole party. But in modern times we would not think of doing that.

While many of the traditional barriers have fallen about which wine goes with which food, some still hold true: a juicy steak will require a full-bodied red wine to stand up to its strong flavor; a more delicate dish, such as simply grilled sole or trout, will be better complemented by a light red or white wine.

The more people in the party, the more flexibility you will have in varying the types of wine served with different courses or entrées. Ordering two bottles or carafes of different types of wine is appropriate when four or five people are dining out together.

As always keep in mind that personal choices are widely variable. A gracious host will always try to accommodate his or her guests' individual tastes and inclinations. And whether one person is paying for the meal or you are dividing the bill,

---

WINE AND FOOD

If you follow these two simple rules of wine and food, you can't go wrong:

• Heavy foods are better complemented by full-bodied wines.

• Lighter fare is best accompanied by lighter wines.

it's a good idea either to know or to ask what different people prefer. A designated driver, for example, will choose to subtract himself or herself from the equation, and if you do not know this beforehand, you may end up ordering and paying for more wine than your party can drink.

The Wine Waiter

In fine restaurants there is a separate waiter called the sommelier, who does nothing but handle wine orders. He or she is distinguished from other waiters by wearing a bunch of keys, a remnant of the days when the sommelier was the only one with a key to the wine cellar.

But in common practice the same waiter who takes your food order will also serve your wine. Many restaurants do, however, train their waiters to be knowledgeable about the wines they offer, and you should follow the same process with the regular waiter as with a sommelier.

The person from whom you order your wine, whether sommelier or waiter, should be familiar with both the wines on the list and how the dishes on the menu are prepared. Tell him or her the style of wine you are considering and the price range you have chosen. Usually the waiter or sommelier will enjoy discussing your choice with you and will make appropriate recommendations.

HOW TO KEEP THE PRICE OF WINE BETWEEN YOU AND THE WAITER

If you want to be discreet, indicate the price level of the wine you are interested in by pointing to it on the menu, rather than saying it out loud.

Opening the Wine

Whether the waiter or sommelier assists you in a restaurant or you do the honors at home, there are certain steps to follow to open your bottle of wine successfully.

The Proper Way to Open a Bottle of Sparkling Wine

Contrary to popular folklore, popping the cork and letting it fly is not the most efficient way to open a bottle of Champagne. Sparkling wines contain natural high pressure, and the cork might hit someone. Opening a bottle in this fashion also wastes the sparkling wine and causes the bubbles to dissipate faster.

Following is the correct way to open a bottle of Champagne or other sparkling wine:

• Remove the foil covering the wire.

• Slant the bottle away from people.

• Carefully loosen and remove the wire hood. Remember that this wire is what has been holding in the pressure of the sparkling wine, so carefully hold onto the cork from now on.

• Grasp the cork firmly and twist the bottle in one direction to remove the cork slowly.

• Gently pour sparkling wine into fluted glasses.

• Caution: never remove the cork from a sparkling wine with a corkscrew.

The Proper Way to Open a Bottle of Still Wine

• Remove the plastic capsule over the cork by cutting under the lip of the rim.
• Wipe any dust or mold from the cork with a clean cloth.

• Use a corkscrew to remove the cork from the bottle. (For information on corkscrews, see the boxed descriptions on page 50.)

Should a Wine Be Allowed to Breathe Before Tasting?

Many wine experts believe that all wine benefits by breathing; others feel that most wine should be opened just prior to tasting. The theory behind allowing a wine to breathe is that when wine is exposed to the air, its interaction with oxygen releases the various compounds that make up its aroma and flavor.

How Long Should a Wine Be Allowed To Breathe?

The amount of time a wine should be exposed to the air, or allowed to breathe, before tasting is a widely debated issue. A taste test will reveal whether a wine is ready to be drunk, or if it needs more time to breathe.

What Wines Benefit Most By Breathing?

Young red wines and some older reds—notably the robust ones, such as Shiraz or Barolo—are probably the wines that benefit most by breathing. As a test, taste a young, tannic red wine when you first open it; the wine is often stiff and unyielding. But taste the same glass of wine again twenty minutes later, and you will often find that it has become smoother through exposure to the air.

Can a Wine Ever Be Damaged By Breathing?

Yes. The most obvious example is Champagne and other sparkling wines. Continued exposure to the air causes them to lose their bubbles.

But other wines as well may not only not benefit, but actually suffer damage, through prolonged exposure to the air. Older Burgundies are a classic case; these excellent but fragile wines lose their flavor when opened too soon before serving.

Try the same taste test with a young white wine as you did

STYLES OF CORKSCREWS

The best corkscrews use leverage to remove the cork from a bottle of wine cleanly and with a minimum of effort.

- Ah-So (Butler's Friend):
  A popular style in California, this corkscrew has two prongs and a handle. Slip the prongs into the bottle on either side of the cork, gently twist, and pull the cork out.

- Screwpull:
  A corkscrew with a knife and a long screw on the end. The cork is easily extracted by turning the corkscrew continuously in one direction.

- T-Bar:
  A T-shaped bar, the top of the T being the handle and the bottom a long screw to insert into the cork. This type of corkscrew, which demands unnecessary effort, is falling out of style.

- Waiter's Friend:
  The top of the bottle is gripped with the "claw" while the cork is leveraged out with the screw.

- Wingtip (Butterfly):
  The screw is inserted into the bottle, and as the top is twisted, the sides of the corkscrew rise up like the wings of a butterfly. Push down the wings of the corkscrew and the cork is removed.

with the young red, and you may get exactly the opposite result. The wine may have more aroma and flavor in its initial exposure to the air and after twenty minutes may become duller.

When Is It Appropriate to Decant a Wine?

Decanting a wine means pouring it into a glass or decanter. It allows a wine to breathe, and is a way to remove the sediment that collects in bottles of older red wines.

Like breathing, decanting is appropriate for certain wines and not for others. A robust Bordeaux may benefit from decanting, growing in flavor and clarity, but the fragile character of a very fine Burgundy may rapidly disintegrate.

If you would like to decant a wine and don't have a decanter on hand, pour a glass out of the bottle and allow the wine to stand for twenty minutes before drinking. Simply removing the cork from the bottle and allowing the bottle to stand open does not significantly help a wine breathe, since only a very small portion of the wine is actually exposed to the air.

Six Basic Steps in Tasting a Wine

Whether you or your waiter has opened your bottle of wine, there are certain classic steps to be followed in tasting it:

- Test the cork
- Swirl the wine
- Look at its color
- Smell the wine
- Taste the wine
- Determine whether the wine has an aftertaste

Test the Cork

A cork should be moist; a dried-out cork suggests that air may have entered the bottle and ruined the wine.

HOW TO DECANT A BOTTLE OF WINE

To decant a bottle of young red wine in order to allow it to breathe, simply pour it into a decanter and pour it back into its original bottle.

To decant a bottle of older red wine with sediment in the bottom, follow these steps:

• Remove the bottle from storage a day before you plan to serve it and stand it upright; this allows the sediment to settle. (Bottles of wine are stored on their sides.)

• When you are ready to serve the wine, remove the cork and wipe the top of the bottle with a clean cloth.

• Set the bottle next to the decanter. A clear crystal decanter is a good choice, in order to best appreciate the color of the wine.

• Holding the neck of the bottle above a good source of light, such as a candle or flashlight, slowly pour the wine from the bottle into the decanter.

• Stop pouring as soon as you see sediment enter the neck of the bottle. The wine in the decanter should be clear, while there will be an inch or so of undrinkable sediment remaining in the wine bottle.

In the rare event that the bottle is "corky"—that is, it smells musty because of a bad cork—the unpleasant odor will be immediately apparent to you. Either return it to the wine store or exchange it for another bottle in the restaurant.

Swirl the Wine

• Swirling wine is a way of exposing it to the oxygen in the air, allowing it to release its full aroma and flavor.

• Sometimes even a good wine has a mild scent of sulphur when it is first opened. Sulphur dioxide is a preservative used in winemaking. But swirling a wine will usually cause this odor to disappear within moments.

• Does the wine have legs? After swirling a rich and full-bodied wine, rivulets called "legs" will run down the sides of the glass.

Look at the Color of the Wine

• Different grapes impart different colors to a wine.

• Aging in wood may impart a deeper hue to a wine.

• White wines tend to darken with age. A young white wine might have a tinge of green; as it ages, the hue may change from straw yellow to gold to amber. Keep in mind, however, that most white wines are meant to be drunk on the young side. Only complex white wines, such as Chardonnays or Sauternes, benefit from aging.

• Complex red wines lighten and gain in clarity with age. In their youth they may be purple or ruby red; as they mellow and mature with age, the color turns lighter, to what wine experts refer to as brick-red.

• The best way to view the color of a wine is against a white background, such as a white piece of paper or a white napkin or tablecloth.

Smell the Wine

• Nose is the term used by wine tasters to describe the bouquet or aroma of a wine.

• The aroma of a young wine is primarily that of the grape from which it was made.

• The bouquet of older wines is a complicated aroma that develops as the various components of a wine age and meld over time.

Taste the Wine

• Roll the wine around on your tongue to take advantage of its full flavor.

• Wine experts like to ''chew'' their wine when tasting it. That is, they slurp it noisily, to combine it with as much oxygen as possible, and then swirl it around in their mouths to release the maximum amount of flavor.

• How does the wine feel on your tongue? What is its weight and texture? Is the wine light-bodied, medium-bodied, full-bodied or robust?

• What is the acidity of a white wine? Too little (flat), too much (tart) or just right?

• Can you detect the tannins in a red or wood-aged white wine? Are they smooth or harsh?

THE FLAVORS OF WINE

• Buttery:
   A smooth texture and rich flavor reminiscent of butter, characteristic of wines that are aged in oak casks.

• Crisp:
   Fresh and lively, with a good acid balance.

- Dry:
  A term used to describe wines in which most or all of the sugar has fermented into alcohol. The opposite of sweet.

- Fruity:
  Having the fresh, springlike flavor and perfume of grapes.

- Herbaceous:
  Having the flavor and aroma of fresh herbs.

- Intense:
  Potent and full-bodied, often with a high alcoholic content.

- Oaky:
  A flavor and aroma in wine imparted by the oak casks in which it was aged.

- Rich:
  Luxurious and full-bodied in bouquet and flavor.

- Robust:
  Big and powerful. Even more forceful and sturdy than full-bodied wines.

- Spicy:
  Having the flavor and aroma of spices such as cinnamon, cloves or pepper.

- Sweet:
  Having a high sugar content. The opposite of dry.

- Velvety:
  Smooth on the tongue.

• Is the wine young or old? Hint: young white wines may be crisp, clean and acidic—this is good. But young red wines may make you pucker up in surprise—when they are too young, the tannins in them make them overly dry.

• What is the flavor of the wine? Is it sweet? Dry? Fruity? If you are not sure of the wine you are sampling, swirl it around in your glass and then sniff and taste it again.

• Is the wine true to its type? For example, is it
  —Robust and intense like a Barolo?
  —Bursting with fresh fruit like a Beaujolais?
  —Velvety rich and full-bodied like a Cabernet Sauvignon?
  —Dry and flinty like a Chablis?
  —Oaky and buttery like a Chardonnay?
  —Spicy like a Gewürztraminer?
  —Dry and crisp like a Macôn-Villages?
  —Sweet and concentrated like a Sauternes?
  —Herbaceous like a Sauvignon Blanc?

The Aftertaste

Aftertaste is the lingering flavor left on the tongue after tasting a fine wine. The aftertaste of a fine wine lasts some twenty seconds or so. Aftertaste is a positive characteristic and stands in contrast to the flat taste that dull, unfinished wines leave on the palate.

The Style of Wine You Are Tasting

The amount of time and attention you pay to tasting a wine is determined by the wine itself. Simple wines naturally require less attention than complex ones; a simple chilled rosé or Beaujolais can be casually quaffed at a picnic, while a mature Bordeaux or Cabernet Sauvignon at a formal dinner demands more concentration.

What Is a Blind Tasting?

A blind tasting is one in which the wine tasters do not know beforehand what types of wines they are tasting or where they come from. This is a fun idea for a party in your home, especially if your appreciation of wine is shared with your friends.

Each person can bring one bottle of wine to the gathering, with the label hidden by a paper bag. Aluminum foil under the paper bag will help to keep white wine cold.

Provide each participant with a glass of water and simple, unsalted crackers to clear the palate between tastes. Then line up several glasses in front of each person, supply everyone with paper and pencil to record his or her impressions of the various wines, and have a good time!

How Much Wine Should Be Poured to Taste?

Whether you are tasting wine at home or in a restaurant, only two to four ounces should be poured into a glass to taste. This provides ample room in which to swirl the wine, allowing its full flavor and bouquet to develop.

How Should a Wineglass Be Held?

A wineglass should be held by the stem. It is awkward to hold it by the base, and holding it by the bowl will alter its temperature.

Does the Type of Glass Wine is Served in Matter?

Yes. Size, shape and color of wineglasses are all important considerations.

• Size:
  A ten- to twelve-ounce glass is best for appreciating the aroma and flavor of wine. Eight-ounce glasses are considered the minimum size, since a smaller size does not allow the wine drinker to swirl the wine and release the subtle complexities that a wine gains over time. Oversized glasses, of sixteen or more ounces, may be clumsy and unwieldy.

• Shape:
  The shape of a wineglass is also important. Tall glasses that taper in at the top allow the full aroma of a wine to be concentrated and captured.

• Color:
  Wineglasses should be clear, so that you can appreciate the color of a wine. Complex white wines darken with age; complex red wines lighten and gain in clarity with age.

Should Different Wines Be Served in Different Glasses?

The all-purpose ten- to twelve-ounce taster's glass is a versatile glass in which any type of wine can be served. However, there are also glasses specifically designed to serve certain types of wine.

Red Wine

Large balloon-shaped glasses are designed to serve red wines. The rich bouquet of red wines can expand in these glasses, which would dwarf the more delicate aroma of a young white wine.

White Wine

Tall, thin glasses that close in toward the top are best for most white wines. They concentrate the aroma of a white wine, which is more delicate than that of a red, and help it stay chilled.

Aromatic White Wine

Hock or Rhine glasses are most suitable for serving aromatic white wines. They have long, thin stems topped by shallow bowls.

Sparkling Wine

The tulip is the best glass in which to serve Champagne and other sparkling wines. Its tall narrow shape helps to retain and concentrate the bubbles.

The saucer glass, or coupe, traditionally used to serve Champagne is actually the worst possible choice. These glasses cause the bubbles to dissipate too quickly.

Tasting Wine in a Restaurant

In addition to the general procedures above, which should be followed in tasting any wine, there are a few special considerations in tasting wine in a restaurant.

* Is the label on the bottle consistent with the wine you ordered?
* Who should taste the wine first?
* When should a wine be sent back?

Read the Label Carefully

This is your opportunity to make sure that the wine you ordered is the wine you are being served. When your waiter shows you the bottle, read the label carefully. Is it the same as the one on the wine list? For example, if you have ordered a recent year, or vintage, of a crisp, acidic white wine—which generally deteriorates with age—and you have received an older year, now is the time to point this out.

Who Should Taste the Wine in a Restaurant?

The host or person who orders the wine is usually the designated taster. But this task can also be passed on to whomever you choose at the table.

A small amount of wine—about two ounces—is poured into the taster's glass. The wine waiter should then wait for the approval of the host or designated taster before proceeding to serve others around the table, and finally return to fill the taster's glass to the appropriate level.

When to Send a Bottle Back

A wine is sent back when there is something wrong with it. If you choose a wine that you don't care for, it's unfortunate, but that alone is not a valid reason to return it. There are cases, however, in which it is appropriate to send back a bottle of wine.

• If the label on the bottle the wine waiter shows you is not the bottle you ordered:

In this case send the bottle back immediately—inform the waiter that this is not the wine you ordered. If that wine is unavailable, make another selection from the wine list.

• If the wine is corky—that is, it smells musty because of a bad cork:

The unpleasant odor should become immediately apparent to both you and the wine waiter. In this case the restaurant should naturally replace the bottle.

• If a white wine is not sufficiently chilled:

In this case you can either send the bottle back to be chilled further or, even simpler, ask the waiter to bring an ice bucket filled with ice and water. The water will speed the process of cooling a wine faster than ice alone. Turn the bottle upside down in the bucket for five minutes to chill, and then call your waiter over to resume the opening ritual.

Is It Appropriate to Refill Your Own Glasses?

Of course! While it's preferable for the waiter to perform this service, if he or she is unavailable, do not hesitate to refill your glass.

Four

Domestic Wines: From California to Rhode Island

Both the quantity and quality of American wines has been on the upswing since the 1970s. Forty states today produce wine. And, led by the vintners in California, Americans have been making increasingly finer wines in the last few decades. In turn, American states have passed laws making it easier for winemakers to produce and market their wines.

Imported, Domestic or Hybrid Grapes?

In the United States there are three types of vines. The indigenous *Vitis labrusca* originally grew wild in the East and is now cultivated there. The European *Vitis vinifera* was first imported to California, and forms the basis of that state's wine industry. And hybrid grapes, a cross between European and American grapes, are grown and made into wine around the country.

Domestic Grapes

Domestic grapes, or grapes that are indigenous to the United States, have what wine experts call a "foxy" (that is, very musky or "grapey") taste that is much different from that of delicate European grapes. *Vitis labrusca* is the name of the type of vine native to the United States. While wine critics note that European grapes make the finest wines, many Americans prefer the unique character of the wines made from our own domestic grapes.

Imported Grapes

More and more American vineyards are being planted with vinifera (imported European, especially French, grape vines), including Chardonnay, Cabernet Sauvignon and Pinot Noir, in place of domestic American grapes. Wine critics consider vinifera to be the grapes from which the finest wine is made. Before the development of modern scientific tools, such as pesticides, these grapes were thought too delicate for many types of American soil and climate.

Hybrid Grapes

European-American hybrids—vines that are a cross between European and native American grapes—combine the delicacy of the vinifera with the sturdiness of domestic labrusca grapes. Many winemakers find them to be the perfect compromise.

INDIGENOUS AMERICAN GRAPES

- Catawba:
  A common vine which produces white grapes. Used for making white and sparkling wines in eastern states, especially New York and Ohio.

- Concord:
  A hardy and adaptable blue-black grape which is the most widely planted in the eastern states. Popular for making sweet kosher wines. Otherwise not used much in winemaking due to its strong foxy taste.

- Diana:

  A delicate vine which produces average white grapes, grown in the Finger Lakes region of New York.

- Diamond:

  Another average grape vine grown in the Finger Lakes region of New York.

- Fredonia:

  A relative of the Concord grape planted primarily in New Jersey.

- Isabella:

  A dark red grape planted in the Finger Lakes region of New York.

- Muscadine:

  A southern grape which has been made into wine for the past four centuries, resulting in the first original wine of the United States. Usually sweetened by winemakers, as otherwise it would taste too harsh. The most common variety of the Muscadine grape is called Scuppernong.

The taste of the wines produced from them is more subtle than that of wines produced from domestic grapes alone, while they have the sturdiness of domestic grapes, which vinifera lack.

Growing hybrids is a less risky proposition for winemakers located in eastern states, where the climate is not so hospitable to vinifera. They are relieved of the worry that a sudden drop in temperature or an unexpected frost will suddenly wipe out a delicate vinifera crop.

Who Makes Domestic Wines?

California makes an overwhelming 90 percent of all domestic wines. In second place is New York, at 7 percent. The oldest winery in the United States is the Brotherhood Winery in New York's Hudson Valley.

Domestic wine producers today range from mom-and-pop operations to the most sophisticated businesses. There are family wineries both large and small.

The winery of brothers Ernest and Julio Gallo is a huge operation which makes almost half the wine of California. In fact one out of every four bottles of American wine sold is made by Gallo. The family-run Cascade Mountain Vineyards of New York, on the other hand, produces small amounts of wine with labels that have included the whimsical "Le Hamburger Red."

Where Are Domestic Wines Made?

Wines are made in nearly every state in the union. Many wines are not widely available outside the area where they are produced; but locally made wines are always a treat, whether they are produced and drunk in a small town in California, New York, Washington or Virginia.

Wineries are also a lot of fun to visit when you travel; most offer—free or for a minimal charge—tours of their premises and a wine tasting. Following is a sample of the domestic wines made in states all around our country.

California

A tour of American winemaking could begin nowhere but California. There are over six hundred vineyards in California, which together make some 70 percent of the wine consumed in the United States.

California produces table wines, sparkling wines and dessert

NEW TRENDS IN DOMESTIC WINES

More American wineries, responding to the concerns of health-conscious Americans, are beginning to produce organic wines. These are wines made from grapes grown without the aid of pesticides. Two of the largest California winemakers, Fetzer and Gallo, are among the participants in this trend.

Another innovation is being pioneered by Glen Ellen: they're experimenting with replacing the traditional cork with a screw cap. While screw caps have always been a familiar sight on bottles of jug wines, Glen Ellen is putting them on higher-quality wines. According to owner Joseph Benziger, the screw top on his light nouveau-style 1990 Dolcetto is to remind customers that this is not a wine to be aged; it should be chilled and drunk tonight.

wines. Winemakers from as far away as New York import California grapes or juice to use in their own wine. California has replaced almost all of the Mission grapes used in its early winemaking with finer European vinifera.

The California Climate

California is graced with a climate and soil ideal for the cultivation of fine vines. While other regions of the country struggle to grow the delicate European vinifera, from which the finest wines are made, conditions in California are naturally equal to those of the great wine regions of the world.

California Grape Names and Styles

Vintners in California started out by labeling their wines according to European place-names. But the names of fine wine-producing regions in France, such as Chablis and Burgundy, have little meaning when applied to wines that are not made there.

Today most good California wines are instead varietals, named for the grape from which they are primarily made. Wine critics agree that the best move made by California vintners was to improve their grape plantings to produce good varietal wines. The movement to emphasize varietals began in the 1940s and 1950s, championed by such well-known names in American wine as Robert Mondavi, Inglenook and Almaden.

Early California winemakers produced powerful and robust reds, often from 100 percent Cabernet Sauvignon. But today the trend is more toward complexity than power; winemakers are experimenting with blends such as Cabernet Sauvignon with Cabernet Franc and Merlot, resulting in wines of greater subtlety and depth.

White Wine

While California Chardonnays are the most well-known white wines, many other grapes are used in this state in the production of white wine. Types of grapes include:

• Chardonnay:
   California Chardonnays are full-bodied, intense and high in alcoholic content, and often have an underlying fruitiness.
      Chardonnay, the premier wine grape of California, is also the premier wine grape of France; there, it is used to make classic white Burgundies such as Chablis and Montrachet. While French wines made from the Chardonnay grape are more balanced by acidity, rich and buttery American Chardonnays are characterized by a complex oakiness due to aging in oak casks.

• Chenin Blanc:
   There are two styles of California Chenin Blanc: dry and off-dry (off-dry means slightly sweet). Both are best drunk when young and fresh. This is the same grape used to make Vouvray in France.

- Gewürztraminer:
  Spicy wines which range from sweet to crisp.

- Sauvignon Blanc:
  Alone it produces a dry wine. In combination with the Sémillon grape it produces a dry California sauterne.

  Sauvignon Blanc is the same grape used, in different proportions with the Sémillon grape, to produce both the dry white Graves wine and sweet white Sauternes of France.

  A brief note to distinguish *Sauternes* from *sauterne:* Sauternes is one of the world's finest sweet wines and is made only in the Sauternes region of France. California sauterne is a dry white wine.

- Sémillon:
  One of the world's finest grapes, it is usually combined with the Sauvignon Blanc grape in California to make a sauterne. Alone it can be made into either a dry or sweet white wine.

Red Wine

California makes red wines from its native grape, Zinfandel, as well as from fine imported European vinifera such as Cabernet Sauvignon and Pinot Noir. Types of grapes include:

- Cabernet Sauvignon:
  The outstanding red wine grape of California. This is the main grape used to make the famous red Bordeaux of France. In California it produces a wine strongly flavored with cassis, or black currant, and cherry, and may also have hints of woodiness or oak imparted by the casks it is aged in.

- Pinot Noir:
  The grape used to make red Burgundy in France. Softer, fruitier and less tannic (or dry) than Cabernet Sauvignon. Thrives in the cooler climates of growing regions in northern California, such as Napa, Sonoma and Mendocino.

- Barbera:
  An Italian grape used in making wines of that name in Italy's renowned Piedmont region. In California rich and full-bodied wines are made from this grape.

- Gamay, Napa Gamay and Gamay Beaujolais:
  Light, fruity and grapey in flavor. Low in the tannin that imparts dryness to wines. An easy wine to drink, best served chilled.

- Merlot:
  California Merlots range from tough and firm to soft and fruity.

- Petite Sirah:
  A variety of California grape originally thought to be the Syrah grape of France's Rhône Valley. Produces dark, full-textured wines reminiscent of those of the Rhône.

- Syrah:
  Some California winemakers are using this Rhône grape to produce muscular Rhône-style red wines.

- Zinfandel:
  Zinfandel is usually considered a native American grape, since no one has successfully been able to trace its history back to Europe. Zinfandel is less complex (and often less expensive) than Cabernet Sauvignon and Pinot Noir, and more intense and alcoholic.
  Some Zinfandels are smooth and elegant; others are full-bodied, powerful and rough-edged. Read the back of the label to see which variety the winemaker has chosen to create.

Rosé Wines, Blush Wines and Vin Gris

- Grenache:
  The grape used to make Tavel rosés in France, it is also used to make rosé wines in California. One of the most

popular California rosés is the Grenache rosé, a light wine, on the sweet side, made by Almaden.

• Pinot Noir:

Pinot Noir is one of the wine grapes being made into a popular new California category, vin gris. Vin gris is a pale dry rosé or blush wine made from red grapes. Sanford Winery makes a dry vin gris from Pinot Noir.

• White Zinfandel:

A popular pale pink, or blush, wine made when the pigment-containing red skins of the Zinfandel grape are removed. Crisp, light and easy to drink.

Sparkling Wine

While the only Champagne that can legally be called true Champagne is made in the Champagne region of France, California winemakers make excellent sparkling wines in the Champagne method, or méthode champenoise.

As mentioned in the earlier discussion of sparkling wine in Chapter One, bubbles are formed when carbon dioxide is trapped in a corked and wired bottle. This takes place through

---

SPARKLING WINE TERMINOLOGY

The terminology used to describe sparkling wines in the United States is based on the French model. Look for these words on the labels:

• Brut:

In France, the driest sparkling wine. Yet the dryness of brut varies among winemakers. Brut California sparkling wines are generally considered less dry than the French wines they are named for.

- Natural, Au Natural or Natur:
  A term used by wineries in the United States whose Natural sparkling wines are drier than their brut variety. Korbel's Natural Champagne and Schramsberg's Natur Blanc de Blancs Reserve Cuvée are excellent entries in this category.

- Extra Dry:
  Paradoxically, extra dry when applied to sparkling wines means sweet.

- Sec:
  Although *sec* means "dry" in French, in the world of sparkling wine it refers to sparkling wine that is sweeter than extra dry.

- Demi-Sec:
  Literally "half-dry," but demi-sec refers to the sweetest style of sparkling wines.

- Blanc de Blancs:
  White sparkling wine made from white grapes, especially Chardonnay.

- Blanc de Noirs:
  White sparkling wine made from red grapes, especially Pinot Noir.

- Crémant:
  A French word which means "creaming," it is used to describe wines that are not fully sparkling.

- Reserve, or Reserve Cuvée:
  Made from the choicest grapes and aged longer than ordinary sparkling wine.

the so-called Champagne method, in which yeast and sugar are added to a bottle of still wine and secondary fermentation takes place in the bottle. The yeast converts the sugar into alcohol, and as the process takes place, carbon dioxide is released.

WINES OF CALIFORNIA

From the Napa Valley
- Beaulieu
- Beringer
- Cakebread
- Carneros Creek
- Caymus
- Christian Brothers
- Clos du Val
- Domaine Chandon
- Freemark Abbey
- Grgich Hills
- Inglenook
- Charles Krug
- Louis Martini
- Robert Mondavi
- Schramsberg
- Sterling

From Sonoma
- Alexander Valley
- Buena Vista
- Château Saint Jean
- Hanzell
- Iron Horse
- Jordan
- Kenwood
- Korbel
- Sebastiani
- Simi
- Sonoma

In California the Chardonnay and Pinot Noir grapes are combined to make the finest sparkling wines. Some of the best known and most renowned names in California sparkling wine are Domaine Chandon, Korbel and Schramsberg.

Wine Regions and Producers

Napa, which is the Indian word for "plenty," is the most famous red wine region of California. Its best grapes are French vinifera: Cabernet Sauvignon closely followed by Pinot Noir.

Sonoma, just north of San Francisco, is second only to Napa in its number of bonded wineries. The Russian River Valley, one of its most noted growing areas, is the site of the vineyards from which Korbel makes its sparkling wine.

In the Mendocino region of northern California grapes are being grown where it was once thought impossible to protect them from the dangers of frost; major winemakers in this area include Fetzer and Parducci.

Alameda County's Livermore Valley is best known for its sauterne-type wines. The largest winery in the world, E. & J. Gallo Company, is located in Modesto.

New York

New York is second to California in domestic wine production. The almost perfect weather enjoyed by the grapes that became New York's 1991 vintage yielded both quality and quantity, and growers believe 1991 may have been their best year ever.

A Difficult Climate for Some Grapes

Although New York has been involved in winemaking longer even than California, its climate was formerly considered inhospitable to European vinifera, the vines which make the finest wines. The seasons of New York until recently have led wine growers to concentrate on indigenous labrusca grapes or European-American hybrids.

Labrusca, Hybrid or Vinifera?

As in many areas around the country, debate rages in
New York's Hudson Valley around which vine to plant. Delicate vinifera, the classic wine vine of Europe, was traditionally considered unable to survive the harsh winters of the
Hudson Valley. Instead winemakers relied on the labrusca
grape and sturdier hybrids, or vines that were a cross between French and native American varieties. Today, how-

---

WINES OF NEW YORK

From the Finger Lakes
- Bully Hill
- Glenora
- Taylor/Great Western
- Wagner

From the Hudson Valley
- Benmarl
- Brotherhood
- Cascade Mountain
- Clinton
- Millbrook
- North Salem
- Rivendell

From Long Island
- Bedell Cellars
- Bridgehampton
- Hargrave
- Lenz
- Palmer Vineyard
- Paumonok
- Southhampton

ever, hybrids, vinifera and indigenous American grapes are all grown in the area. Many winemakers are holding their breath, waiting to see how the vinifera will fare in the Hudson Valley.

Wine Regions and Producers

Three major growing regions of New York are the Finger Lakes, the Hudson Valley and Long Island. Most large winemakers can be found in the Finger Lakes region, but on Long Island newer vineyards take advantage of the fact that they have a growing season forty-five days longer than that in the Finger Lakes. Long Island winemakers, using the Cabernet Franc, Cabernet Sauvignon and Merlot grapes, are producing sophisticated Bordeaux-style red wines.

The oldest surviving wineries in the country, dating back to the early 1800s, include Benmarl and Brotherhood in the Hudson Valley. In fact, the Hudson Valley's first vines were planted by the Huguenots in 1677. But only in the 1970s, three hundred years after the original endeavor, did winemaking become successful and important in New York.

Other Middle Atlantic States

In spite of their similar climates, the wine industries of Maryland, New Jersey and Pennsylvania each acquired its own unique character.

Maryland

It was in Maryland that the famous native American grape, Catawba, was discovered. Today wineries in Maryland produce wines primarily from French-American hybrid grapes. In fact, it was the founders of the Boordy Vineyard in Maryland who introduced French hybrids commercially to the United States in 1945. They proved that a good eastern American wine could be made from hybrid grapes.

New Jersey

Dr. Thomas Welch first started growing Concord grapes for his famous grapes and jellies in New Jersey and moved to the Finger Lakes region of New York only after his crop was ruined by grape rot in the late 1800s. But not far from the boardwalk of Atlantic City is one of the oldest continuously operating wineries in the country. The Renault Winery of New Jersey survived Prohibition by producing a very popular nerve tonic and selling it in drugstores; the fact that the "Renault Wine Tonic" had an alcoholic content of 22 percent—in an otherwise dry country—probably contributed to its popularity!

Pennsylvania

William Penn first brought European grapes to the Philadelphia area in the late 1600s. But the cultivation of grapes in Pennsylvania has been largely limited to the Concord grape, which is more suitable for making jams and jellies than wine. Pennsylvania's wine industry, moreover, did not receive any extra incentive when Prohibition ended; until 1968 state laws

---

WINES OF THE MIDDLE ATLANTIC STATES

- Alba (NJ)
- Boordy (MD)
- Bucks County (PA)
- Byrd (MD)
- Catoctin (MD)
- Chaddsford (PA)
- Montbray (MD)
- Nissley (PA)
- Renault (NJ)
- Tewksbury (NJ)
- Tomasello (NJ)

still prohibited the sale of alcoholic beverages in anywhere other than state stores.

New England

It is only recently—in the last twenty years—that New England has seriously entered the domestic wine arena. But wild domestic grapes always grew well in New England. Martha's Vineyard in Massachusetts was named for them, and the Concord grape was named after the town of Concord in the same state. While New England wines are not yet well known throughout the country, they are proudly displayed in wine stores and on restaurant wine lists in that area.

Labrusca, Hybrids or Vinifera?

Today winemakers in New England have begun to cultivate more classic wine grapes; they have started to replace some of the acres planted with labrusca grapes native to the United States with imported European vinifera and French-American hybrid grapes.

Wine Regions and Producers

While there are vineyards throughout New England, most are in Connecticut, followed by Rhode Island and Massachu-

---

WINES OF NEW ENGLAND

- Bartlett Estate (ME)
- Chamard (CT)
- Chicama (MA)
- Crosswoods (CT)
- Haight (CT)
- Hopkins (CT)
- Prudence Island (RI)
- Sakonnet (RI)

setts. Many of the new vineyards are located in coastal areas, where the moderating influence of ocean breezes provides some protection from harsh New England winters. Two of the vineyards—Prudence Island in the Narragansett Bay of Rhode Island and Chicama on Martha's Vineyard in Massachusetts— are actually located on offshore islands.

The South

Winemakers scattered through states around the South usually make wine from the area's indigenous Muscadine grape. The exception is Virginia, the region's leading state in both the quantity and quality of the wine it produces.

Virginia

Virginia was the first colony to produce wine in the New World. Long ago Thomas Jefferson attempted to grow classic French grapes, or vinifera, at his home in Monticello. While he was unsuccessful at that time, today vinifera grapes thrive

---

WINES OF THE SOUTH

- Barboursville (VA)
- Biltmore Estate (NC)
- Burnley (VA)
- Ingleside Plantation (VA)
- Lafayette (FL)
- Laurel Hill (TN)
- Linden (VA)
- Misty Mountain (VA)
- Naked Mountain (VA)
- Oakencroft (VA)
- Piedmont (VA)
- Stonewall (VA)
- Wiederkehr (AK)
- Williamsburg (VA)

in Virginia. Modern science has come up with ways to thwart
the pests and the moisture that destroyed vinifera grapes in
Thomas Jefferson's time, and Virginia, with more than forty
vineyards, is now the most important winemaking state in the
South.

Grapes of the South: Muscadines

Elsewhere in the region most wines are made from grapes
native to the United States called Muscadines. Muscadines,
made into wine for the past four centuries, resulted in the first
original wine of the United States.

Wines made with Muscadine grapes—the most common variety of which is Scuppernong—are usually sweetened by
winemakers, as otherwise they would taste too harsh. Newer
vineyards are beginning to replace Scuppernongs with Muscadine hybrids, such as Carlos, Dixie, Magnolia and Noble.

The Midwest

Before Prohibition and the Depression, the Midwest was a major wine-producing region. Many winemakers there in the
1800s were Italian and German immigrants who carried their
crafts to the United States from their native lands.

A Winery in the Midwest

The story of the Stone Hill Winery of Missouri is a micro-
cosm of the history of winemaking in the Midwest. Started in
1847 by an enterprising German immigrant named Michael
Poeschel, by 1900 Stone Hill was the second largest winery
in the United States and the third largest in the world, annually
producing more than a million gallons of wine.

Prohibition and the Depression brought this era to an end,
and only mushrooms were cultivated at Stone Hill until 1965.
Then a renewed interest in wine production spurred a local
couple to buy Stone Hill and restore it to its original purpose.

```
┌─────────────────────────────────────────────┐
│                                               │
│        WINES OF THE MIDWEST                   │
│         • Alexis Bailly (MN)                  │
│         • Alto (IL)                           │
│         • Boskydel (MI)                       │
│         • Fenn Valley (MI)                    │
│         • Good Harbor (MI)                    │
│         • Hermannhof (MS)                     │
│         • Huber (IN)                          │
│         • Lynfred (IL)                        │
│         • Markko (OH)                         │
│         • Meier's (OH)                        │
│         • Mount Pleasant (MS)                 │
│         • Oliver (IN)                         │
│         • St. Julian (MI)                     │
│         • Stone Hill (MS)                     │
│         • Wollersheim (WI)                    │
│                                               │
└─────────────────────────────────────────────┘
```

The Southwest

As in the Midwest, the winemaking industry of the Southwest was battered by Prohibition and the Depression. Today this emerging wine region shows great hope for the future.

Texas

While Texas had many vineyards in the 1800s, by the early 1970s only one remained. In 1974, however, Texas A & M University came out with a study proclaiming that Texas had growing conditions appropriate for the cultivation of grapes. Soon wineries began to spring up all over Texas.

Other Southwestern States

Soon more Southwestern states joined in the renaissance of winemaking in the region. New Mexico's wine history dates back to the 1600s, when wine was produced for religious purposes by Spanish colonists. Today the famous Four Corners region—where the states of New Mexico, Arizona, Utah and Colorado converge—is a noted winemaking area.

WINES OF THE SOUTHWEST

- Anderson Valley (NM)
- Blue Teal (NM)
- Fall Creek (TX)
- Llano Estacado (TX)
- Messina Hof (TX)
- Pheasant Ridge (TX)
- Rio Valley (NM)
- Sonoita (AZ)
- Val Verde (TX)

The Northwest

The Northwest is hot on the heels of California in wine production. These states are beginning to take their place alongside California as makers of premium wines.

Washington

Washington is now the third largest producer of wine in the United States, and the second largest domestic producer of the classic wines made from imported European vinifera grapes. Only about a third of the acreage suitable for growing wine grapes in Washington has been used so far, leaving open the possibility of tremendous future expansion. The Yakima Valley is the major wine-producing area of Washington.

Other Northwestern States

Idaho's wine production is still in the early stages, often using grapes from nearby Washington. But Oregon has already scored a major success with its velvety and full-bodied Pinot Noirs. The finest domestic Pinot Noirs—round, soft red wines made from the grape of the same name—are made in California and Oregon. The entry of Robert Drouhin of Burgundy, France, into Oregon's Willamette Valley has given a great lift to that state's wine industry.

WINES OF THE NORTHWEST

- Camas (ID)
- Château Ste. Michelle (WA)
- Columbia Crest (WA)
- Domaine Drouhin (OR)
- Hillcrest (OR)
- F.W. Langguth (WA)
- Oak Knoll (OR)
- Panther Creek (OR)
- Preston (WA)
- Quail Run (WA)
- Ste. Chapelle (ID)
- Paul Thomas (WA)

Five

The Wines of France

France produces and exports some of the finest wines in the world. The French are also great lovers of their own wine; while Americans consume a little over two gallons per person annually, the French drink almost twenty! In fact some 10 percent of the average French family's budget is spent on wine.

The Two Categories of French Wine

- Vin Ordinaire:
  Simple wine. The vast majority of French wine, "ordinaire," is made for everyday drinking. Includes 85 percent of all French wine.

- Appellation d'Origine Contrôlée (AOC):
  Complex wine. The Appellation d'Origine Contrôlée (AOC) is the branch of the French government that regulates the wine industry and sets minimum standards for the fine wines of France. Only 15 percent of all French wine meets the strict requirements of the AOC.

The Wine Regions of France

With the exception of Alsace, which labels its wines according to grape variety, French wines are named after the region in which they are made. Following are a selection of the major wine regions of France, and descriptions of some of the wines made in them.

The Wines of Bordeaux

Bordeaux may well be the most important wine region of France. Bordeaux produces wines of outstanding quality and in more quantity than any other area. Its important wine regions—or, in French, *appellations contrôlées*—include Sauternes, Barsac, Médoc, Pomerol, Saint-Emilion and Graves.

The Vintages of Bordeaux

Vintages are very much emphasized in Bordeaux wines. Better weather results in better vintages. Recent recommended vintages are 1982, 1983, 1985, 1986, 1988, 1989 and 1990.

Red Bordeaux

These are among the finest wines in the world—in fact *the* finest according to many wine critics. Although there is a wide range of red wine in Bordeaux, they share a longevity (they last and age well) and a unique earthy smell evocative of violets. With age a red Bordeaux grows in softness and subtlety. Letting the wine breathe before serving adds to its flavor and bouquet.

- The Châteaux of Bordeaux:
  Red Bordeaux has also been known by its English name, claret, for the last seven centuries. Neither Bordeaux nor claret, however, will appear on the label of this wine. Bordeaux wines are usually named for the château, or estate, in which they are made.
  Some of the great châteaux of Bordeaux include Château Haut-Brion, Château Lafite-Rothschild, Château

Latour, Château Margaux and Château Mouton-Rothschild.

• The Regions and Grapes of Red Bordeaux:

The four great red Bordeaux regions are Médoc, Graves, Saint-Emilion and Pomerol. In the Médoc region are four important inner appellations: Margaux, Pauillac, Saint-Estèphe and Saint-Julien. Most red Bordeaux is made from the Cabernet Sauvignon, Merlot and Cabernet Franc grapes.

White Bordeaux

The best dry white Bordeaux comes from the Graves region of France, and the best wines of Graves in turn carry the name of the château in which they are made. These wines are dry, light and crisp, with a good acid balance; they may also be fruity, herbaceous or grassy in flavor and bouquet.

• Reading a White Bordeaux Label:

If "Graves" appears unaccompanied by the name of the château on the label, the wine is the lowest category of white Bordeaux, but this is usually still a good wine and the price will be lower than château-bottled Bordeaux. The white Bordeaux of Entre-Deux-Mers, another district of the region, is often a bargain; it is mellow, soft and dry. White Bordeaux is made primarily from the Sauvignon Blanc grape.

• Sauternes:

Sauternes is the sweet white Bordeaux from the Sauternes region of France. This is a sublime dessert wine, made from Sémillon grapes gathered late in the season when they have become overripe. The grapes are allowed to enter a state of "noble rot," or *Botrytis cinerea,* in which they wither, natural acids are reduced, and natural sugars and juices are concentrated. The process is a risky and expensive one, resulting in excellent wines with very steep price tags attached. Sauternes will live longer, or outlast, the other white wines of France. The most famous French Sauternes is that of Château d'Yquem.

HOW BORDEAUX HELPED A HOSTAGE KEEP HIS SANITY

French journalist Jean-Paul Kauffmann was a hostage in Lebanon for three years, from 1985 to 1988. In the wine magazine *L'Amateur*, which he launched upon his release, he told how he kept his sanity during captivity by nightly reciting the sixty-one properties that make up the 1855 classification of the châteaus of Bordeaux.

The Wines of Burgundy

Burgundy may be one of the most widely misapplied wine names in the world. Real Burgundy comes only from the region of France of the same name, but bottles of heavy, dark red wine from around the world are often labeled as Burgundy. In fact some of the greatest Burgundies are white, and true red Burgundies range from the light and fruity Beaujolais to the delicate wines of Pommard and Beaune.

- **What Makes Burgundy Such Great Wine?**
  The producers of Burgundy wines consider their soil and the slope of their land the most important elements in making quality wines. These determine the level of excellence which a wine reaches: in ascending order, a village wine, a prémier cru or a grand cru.

Red Burgundy

Red Burgundy challenges red Bordeaux for the title of world's finest wine, and each side has its proponents. Red Burgundy is a complex wine of exquisite silkiness and softness. The primary grape used in its production is the Pinot Noir.

- **The Vintages of Red Burgundy:**
  Vintages are particularly important in Burgundy, where uncertain weather makes some years noticeably better

or worse than others. Recent good vintages include
1978, 1979, 1981, 1983, 1985, 1988 and 1989.

• The High Price of Burgundy:
The laws of supply and demand have combined to drive
up the price of Burgundy. From this small region with
its erratic weather come some of the finest wines in the
world, and it seems as if everyone wants them. While
good weather in recent years has resulted in bigger
crops, Burgundy still produces only about a sixth as
much first-quality wine as Bordeaux.

• Wine Labels and Shippers:
As a general rule, the more detailed the label, the finer
and therefore the more expensive the wine. Look also
on the label for the names of reliable shippers of red
Burgundies; they include Bouchard Père & Fils, Joseph
Drouhin, Louis Jadot and Louis Latour.

• The Famous Red Wine Regions of Burgundy:
Unlike Bordeaux, Burgundies are not named for châteaus. They are named for the regions in which they are
produced. The major red Burgundy region is the Côte
d'Or, which is divided into the Côte de Beaune and the
Côte de Nuits. The Côte de Beaune region produces
delicate red Burgundies such as Beaune, Pommard and
Volnay. The Côte de Nuits is the home of the biggest,
full-bodied red Burgundies. Among the many names to
look for are Le Chambertin, Clos de la Roche, Eché-
zeaux, Les Grands-Echézeaux, Le Musigny, Nuits-
Saint-Georges and Richebourg.

Beaujolais
A simple, fresh, fruity, young red wine made from the Gamay grape in Burgundy. Drink it slightly chilled. Georges Duboeuf is known as the King of Beaujolais, and it is always
safe to buy a bottle of Beaujolais with his name on it. Other
reliable shippers include Joseph Drouhin, Louis Jadot and Di-
dier Mommessin.
The best Beaujolais is not necessarily labeled Beaujolais. As

THE THREE CATEGORIES OF BEAUJOLAIS

- Beaujolais:
  The basic Beaujolais, which accounts for most of the Beaujolais produced. Drink within a year.

- Beaujolais-Villages:
  One step up from Beaujolais, a blend of wines from the thirty-five villages that consistently produce the best Beaujolais. Drink within a year or two.

- Cru Beaujolais:
  The best Beaujolais, named for one of the nine villages in which it is made. More expensive than the other types and lasts a number of years longer in the bottle.

mentioned in Chapter Two, it is often called Cru Beaujolais and is named for one of the following villages in which it is made: Brouilly, Chénas, Chiroubles, Côte de Brouilly, Fleurie, Juliénas, Morgon, Moulin-à-Vent and Saint-Amour.

Beaujolais Nouveau

Beaujolais Nouveau—not to be confused with regular Beaujolais—is a unique wine, bottled when it is only days old and sold only weeks after that.

- How Is Beaujolais Nouveau Made?
  This simple, fresh and fragrant young purple wine is made by carbonic maceration; that is, to capture the full aroma and fragrance of Gamay grapes just days after their harvest, whole grapes are fermented under carbon dioxide in a tank.

- **When Is Beaujolais Nouveau Available?**
  Each November Beaujolais Nouveau (or New Beaujolais) appears in wine stores and restaurants. Drink it chilled. Beaujolais Nouveau should be consumed within six months of purchase; it is at its best soon after bottling.

  ## White Burgundy

  When the name appears alone, *Burgundy* usually refers to red Burgundy. But white Burgundy is also numbered among the finest wines in the world. White Burgundies are full-bodied, complex wines. They are dry and, at their best, possess an exquisite acid balance. The 1989 vintage of white Burgundy is considered outstanding.

- **The Grapes of White Burgundy:**
  All white Burgundies are made from 100 percent Chardonnay grapes. American Chardonnays are patterned after white Burgundies, as they are made from the same elegant grape.

- **White Burgundy Producers:**
  From roughly least to most expensive, white Burgundies include Macôn-Villages, Macôn Blanc, Puligny-Montrachet, Chassagne-Montrachet, Corton-Charlemagne, Bâtard-Montrachet and Le Montrachet.

- **The Famous White Wine Regions of Burgundy:**
  The three major white Burgundy regions are Chablis, Côte de Beaune and Mâconnais.
  The small Chablis region produces Chablis, an elegant dry and flinty white wine. The three levels of Chablis are, from least to most expensive: Chablis, Chablis Premier Cru and Chablis Grand Cru. Names of shippers to look for include Albert Pic & Fils, Joseph Drouhin, J. Moreau & Fils and Louis Jadot.
  Most wines from the Côte de Beaune area are red, but three of the finest are complex full-bodied white wines: Chassagne-Montrachet, Meursault and Puligny-Montrachet.

Mâconnais is the region's producer of simple dry white wines. Pleasant, light and reliable, they include Mâcon Blanc, Mâcon-Villages, St.-Véran and Pouilly-Fuissé.

Champagne

The only true Champagne—Champagne with a capital *C*—comes from the sixty-thousand-acre Champagne region of France. There, Pinot Noir and Chardonnay vines are grown and made into a delicious sparkling wine in accordance with strict French laws.

The Legend of Dom Pérignon

A famous legend in Champagne country is that of the Benedictine monk Dom Pérignon. "I've been drinking stars!" he exclaimed one day of Champagne. In the seventeenth century he revolutionized the industry by using a heavier bottle for Champagne. Before that Champagne's carbon dioxide bubbles would expand and cause ordinary thinner bottles to explode. Today one of the finest Champagnes of the region, Dom Pérignon of Moët & Chandon, is named for the resourceful monk.

Vintage or Non-Vintage Bubbles?

All Champagne should be served chilled, at around forty degrees Fahrenheit. To preserve the bubbles, it is best served in tulip-shaped rather than saucer glasses. The French make a distinction between vintage and non-vintage Champagnes; vintages are declared by some houses in their best years. But vintage Champagnes are more expensive than non-vintage ones, which are actually more typical of the house style than vintage Champagnes.

Some Famous Champagne Houses

As Bordeaux wine is usually named for the château, or estate, in which it is made, Champagne is named for the *house* in which it is made. There are more than 130 Champagne houses in France. Some of the most famous include Bollinger, Moët & Chandon, Mumm, Perrier-Jouët, Piper-Heidsieck, Pol Roger, Pommery & Greno, Louis Roederer, Ruinart, Taittinger and Veuve Clicquot.

CHAMPAGNE TERMINOLOGY

Following are some terms commonly found on the labels of French Champagne:

- Brut:
  The driest Champagne of France.

- Extra Dry:
  Paradoxically, extra dry when applied to sparkling wines means sweet.

- Sec:
  Although *sec* means "dry" in French, on a Champagne label it means sweeter than extra dry.

- Demi-Sec:
  Literally "half-dry," but demi-sec is the sweetest style of Champagne.

- Blanc de Blancs:
  White Champagne made from white grapes, especially Chardonnay.

- Blanc de Noirs:
  White Champagne made from red grapes, especially Pinot Noir.

- Crémant:
  A French word, which means "creaming," it is used to describe wines that are not fully sparkling.

- Reserve or Reserve Cuvée:
  Made from the choicest grapes and aged longer than ordinary Champagne or other sparkling wine.

Alsace

The wines of Alsace are white and dry. Unlike other French wine, which is named for its region of origin, Alsace wine is labeled by grape variety, and must contain 100 percent of the grape after which it is named.

The Grapes of Alsace

The grapes of Alsace are the same used in neighboring Germany: Riesling, Gewürztraminer and Pinot Blanc. But the wines made from the same grapes are very different. Alsace vintners allow all the sugar in the grapes to ferment, resulting in a dry wine; in contrast, the typical German style is to add some of the naturally sweet unfermented juice to their wines, resulting in sweeter flavors.

The Best Shippers of Alsace Wines

The average plot of an Alsatian grower is only three acres, so it is not economically feasible for them to produce and market their own wines. Therefore they sell their grapes to shippers, who also bottle them.

Reliable names to look for in shipping Alsace wines are Léon Beyer, Dopff & Irion, Hugel Père & Fils and Trimbach.

The Three Major White Wines of Alsace

• Gewürztraminer:
  Gewürz is the German word for spice, and these dry white wines are distinctively spicy.

• Pinot Blanc
  A simple dry white wine, characteristically round and soft.

• Riesling
  The dry white wine considered the best of Alsace.

The Loire Valley

Like Alsace, the Loire Valley produces mainly dry white wines. Also like Alsace, the region produces wines that are usually reasonably priced. They are meant to be drunk on the young side.

The Major White Wines of the Loire Valley

• Muscadet:
  A crisp, light-bodied dry wine, made from the Melon grape. Best drunk when one to two years old.

• Pouilly-Fumé:
  The most full-bodied of the Loire wines, made from the Sauvignon Blanc grape. Best drunk when three to five years old.

• Sancerre:
  Crisp, herby and drier than Pouilly-Fumé. Also made from the Sauvignon Blanc grape. Best drunk when two to three years old.

• Vouvray:
  A semi-dry white wine, which can last several years longer than the other Loire wines. It has just a touch of sweetness. Made from the Sauvignon Blanc grape.

The Rhône Valley

Wines from France's Rhône Valley constitute some of the best values in French wines. The primary grape is the Syrah, which produces firm and robust red wines. Rhône wines are usually bigger, fuller wines than Burgundies, with a higher alcoholic content. Ninety-five percent of wines made in the Rhône Valley are red. Experts such as Robert Parker consider them "the world's most underrated wines."

The Major Red Wines of the Rhône Valley

• Chateauneuf-du-Pape:
  A full-bodied red wine, at its best when between five and ten years old. Deep-colored and softer than many other Rhône wines. Made primarily from the Grenache and Syrah grapes.

- Côte Rôtie:
  French for "Roasted Slope," a robust and heady red
  wine. Rich in color, with a hint of violet in the bouquet.
  Some wine critics feel that Côte Rôtie is the best Rhône
  wine. Made solely from the Syrah grape.

- Côtes-du-Rhône:
  The simple rough and ready red wines that are one of
  the best values on the French wine scene today. Robust,
  sturdy and heady. Made from a blend of the region's
  grapes.

- Crozes-Hermitage:
  One of the biggest, fullest wines of the northern Rhône
  Valley. Made solely from the Syrah grape.

- Hermitage:
  Another candidate for best Rhône wine, Hermitage red
  wine is full-bodied and robust when young, acquiring
  more softness as it ages. Exceptional vintages of Hermitage can last fifty years. Made solely from the Syrah
  grape.

- Tavel
  Tavel is one of the best French rosé wines. Made from
  the Grenache grape, it is light, dry and refreshing. Best
  served chilled.

Six

More Wines of the World: From Argentina to Spain

The thirst for wine is as old as civilization itself. The Code of Hammurabi, who was King of Babylon in almost 1800 B.C., regulated the sale of wine in a way similar to laws currently in use in many countries.

Today wine is made by countries throughout the world. But the types of wine each country produces, their quality, the rate of domestic consumption and the amount each country exports are all widely variable. Following is a sampling of the some of the international wines available to American wine drinkers.

ARGENTINA

Argentina is the largest South American producer of wine, and the fourth largest producer of wine worldwide, following only Italy, France and Spain. Not surprisingly, the people of Argentina also drink a lot of wine, trailing only France and Italy in their annual rate of consumption. While Chile now produces more quality wines than Argentina, some excellent bargains can be found in Argentinian wines.

South American Bargains

Argentinian wines, like those of Chile, are gaining increasing popularity in the United States. They can often be found for under ten dollars and represent good value for your money.

Wine Regions and Producers

Among the best choices of Argentinian wines are the red Cabernet Sauvignons and the white Chardonnays. The states of Mendoza and San Juan are graced with a soil and climate ideal for the production of wine. Look for brand names such as Navarro Correas and Trapiche.

AUSTRALIA

Wines from this country entered the American consciousness with an impact similar to the hit Australian move *Crocodile Dundee.* In the 1980s it became very fashionable to serve your guests the red Shiraz wines of Australia, which are similar in taste and character to Cabernet Sauvignons. At their best both are full-bodied, deeply colored and powerful wines.

A Climate Like California's

The best vineyards of both Australia and California lie at about the same altitude and have climates similarly beneficial to the production of wine. While Australian wines are often compared to California wines, most wine critics give California the edge.

Australian Grape Names

Another parallel between Australian and Californian wine-making is that vintners in both locations began by labeling their wines according to European place-names. But the names of fine wine-producing regions in France, such as Chablis and Burgundy, have little meaning when applied to wines that are not made there. Most good Australian wines, like American ones, are now named for the grape from which they are made.

Red Wines

The best Australian red wines carry varietal names such as Shiraz (the Australian equivalent of the Syrah grape used in the Rhône wines of France) and Cabernet Sauvignon. Often these two grapes are blended by winemakers, resulting in rich, complex and full-bodied wines. Shiraz grapes can lend a smoky or spicy flavor to the wine.

- Cabernet Sauvignon:
  Australian Cabernets range from simple, smooth and fruity to complex, rich and intense. In general they are less robust than wines made with Australia's Shiraz grape. Best drunk when three to five years old.

- Cabernet/Shiraz:
  Alternatively called Shiraz/Cabernet, a blend of Cabernet Sauvignon and Shiraz grapes which usually results in a simple, fruity and robust red wine. Best drunk when two to four years old. Other grapes, such as Merlot and Malbec, may also be used.

- Shiraz:
  The strongest, brawniest Australian red. Can be smoky or spicy. Shiraz is the Australian name for the Syrah grape of France's Rhône Valley. It is actually the Persian translation of Syrah. Sometimes called Hermitage, which is also name of the finest Rhône wine made from the Syrah grape. Many Shiraz wines fit into the category of complex, full-bodied red wines. Their tannic nature requires aging, preferably for at least three to five years.

White Wines

Sémillon, Chardonnay, Sauvignon Blanc and Rhine Riesling are names of grapes to look for in Australian white wines. As in the red wines, these white wine grapes are often blended by winemakers. A Sémillon-Chardonnay, for example, combines the rich, soft, full character of the Sémillon with the intense crispness of the Chardonnay.

- Chardonnay:
  A complex and full-flavored white wine, oaky and fruity, often scented with an aroma of apples or vanilla.

Rich and buttery. More similar to American Chardonnays than to French wines made from the Chardonnay grape, which are drier. Benefits from aging, preferably for at least one to three years.

• Rhine Riesling:
An aromatic white wine, also known as Riesling or Johannisberg Riesling, produced from Germany's Johannisberg Riesling grape. Lightweight, low in alcohol, with a flowery bouquet. Dry or off-dry in taste. Ready to drink when a year or two old, although it can last much longer.

• Sauvignon Blanc:
A simple white wine, crisp and acidic. May be herbaceous, grassy or lemony. Meant to be drunk on the young side, when a year or two old. In Australia, as in the United States, often goes by the name of Fumé Blanc. Benefits from being served chilled.

• Sémillon:
One of Australia's most popular white grapes, Sémillon is rich, ripe and fruity. Alone it is somewhat aromatic. Often blended with Chardonnay or Sauvignon grapes, which balance the aromatic nature of Sémillon with their relative crispness and acidity. Most Sémillons are drunk on the young side, but improve in quality if allowed to age a few years.

Wine Regions and Producers

A good rule of thumb to follow in choosing an Australian wine is to remember that the higher-quality wines are named after grapes rather than regions. However, as consumers grow more familiar with the most famous wine regions, such as Coonawarra and Hunter Valley in the south and Clare Watervale in northern Australia, these local names are taking a more prominent place on labels. Among the most well-known and reliable producers of wine in Australia are Brown Brothers, Thomas Hardy & Sons, Penfold's, Rosemount and Tyrrell.

AUSTRIA

Austrian winemaking goes back a thousand years, but Austrian wines are not that easy to find in the United States. The reason? Austrians drink most of their own wine.

White Wines

Almost all Austrian wine is white. Labeled according to the names of the villages they come from and often the grapes from which they are made, the wines of Austria are usually light and crisp. They include wines with forbidding names such as Schluck—but once you get beyond the unfamiliar name you will find yourself with a simple dry, white wine.

Austrian Grapes

If you see terms such as Spätlese and Auslese on an Austrian wine label, the wine is made from riper grapes picked later in the season, resulting in a sweeter wine. The sweetest and most expensive wine in this category is Eiswein.

Austrian Wines and German Terminology

Austria uses the same grapes and some of the same terminology that Germany uses to describe its wines, including Spätlese, Auslese, Beerenauslese and Trockenbeerenauslese. But Austrian laws are not as strict as those of Germany; as a result the wines are not so sweet as their German counterparts. They are often less expensive than German wines and can represent a better value for your money.

Reading an Austrian Wine Label

A rating system categorizes Austrian wines, and this information is included on their wine labels. The wines range from the semi-dry Kabinett to the sweetest Eiswein. For a more detailed description of the terms you will find on Austrian wine labels, turn to the section on German wines later in this chapter.

Wine Regions and Producers

Some of the best dry white wine of Austria hails from its Wachau region. Other notable place-names include Gumpold-skirchen, Krems, Langenlois and Rust. Notable Austrian wine producers include Friz Salomon and Siegendorf.

CHILE

South American wines are good bargains, and Chile's wine industry is one of the best regulated in the world. Spaniards began to plant vineyards in Chile when they first explored the country, and by the middle of the nineteenth century the French were also making wine in Chile. In fact the famous Château Lafite-Rothschild has entered into a union with the owners of the Los Vascos winery in Chile, whose families have owned the vineyard since 1760.

An Ideal Climate for Wine

Chile has a climate very harmonious to the making of wine. The summers are seldom excessively hot. The soil is rich, and water from the melted snow of the Andes provides natural irrigation to many vineyards.

Red Wines

Cabernet Sauvignon is the premier red-wine grape of Chile. Chile's Cabernets are intense wines, with the rich flavor of fruit and a hint of oak from the casks in which they are aged. Often Cabernet Sauvignon is blended with other red-wine grapes, such as Merlot. The Cabernet Sauvignon provides complexity and longevity, while Merlot offers softness and elegance.

White Wines

Chilean winemakers use the Riesling, Sauvignon Blanc and Sémillon grapes in their white wines. One of the best Chilean wines is the Riesling, but since this grape is expensive to grow, the wines made from it may be hard to find. A wonderful buy is often found in the Sauvignon Blancs of Chile; wines of crisp fruit flavor and acidity, they are usually priced under ten dollars.

How to Read a Wine Label from Chile

Chilean wine labels include the name of the grape, the producer of the wine and the region where the wine was made. The year of the wine may be included on the label, or you may encounter one of these terms:

- Special:
  Aged at least two years.

- Reservado:
  Aged at least four years.

- Gran Viño:
  Aged at least six years.

Wine Regions and Producers

The Maipo Valley is Chile's finest wine-producing region. It is closely followed by the Aconcagua Valley, which is located in the same central region. Names to look for in Chilean wines are Canepa, Concha y Toro, Los Vascos and Undurraga.

GERMANY

Germany produces some of the finest wines in the world. But German wine labels, inscribed with ornate Gothic script, have typically been the most obscure and difficult to find your way around. Before a law was passed simplifying labels in 1971, one of some thirty thousand vineyards, or *einzellagen*, could be found on the label of each bottle. The 1971 labeling laws reduced that number to a still-hefty three thousand.

The Style of German Wines

German wines are generally sweet, balanced with some acidity, and low in alcohol. German wines average 8 to 10 percent in alcoholic content, in contrast to 11 to 13 percent in French wines. In response to an American preference for somewhat drier wines, Germany has begun producing and exporting more *trocken* (dry) and *halb-trocken* (semi-dry) wines to this country. Blue Nun, a semi-sweet Liebfraumilch (Translation: "Milk of the Blessed Mother"), is a popular wine in this category.

Categories of White Wine

Most German wines—and all of the finest German wines—are white. They are classified on the label as either *Tafelwein* or *Qualitätswein*. The exact translation of Tafelwein is "table wine," and in Germany this classification refers to a category of wine that is simple and uncomplicated. Qualitätswein, or quality wine, must come from a designated quality region and have a minimum percentage of alcohol. German quality wines are finer than table wines, and more expensive.

German Wine Grapes and Regions

The best German wine grape is the Johannisberg Riesling. Riesling grape vines are resistant to cold and ripen late in the season. They yield small amounts of wine of great character and delicate, perfumey bouquet. The finest German wines—the Spätlesen, Auslesen, Trockenbeerenauslesen and Eisweins—are made from the Riesling grape.

Other German wine grapes include the spicy Gewürztraminer, the Müller-Thurgau and the Sylvaner.

The two major wine-producing regions of Germany are the Rhine and the Moselle.

Sweet German Wines

There are two processes through which Germany produces its sweet wines. The first is simpler and more economical; the second is very expensive and reserved for the finest wines.

• Most German wines are first fermented dry. Then German winemakers add naturally sweet unfermented juice, which they have held in reserve, producing a sweeter flavor. This process is called chaptalisation.

• The finest German sweet wines, such as Trockenbeerenauslesen and Eiswein, are made from grapes gathered late in the season, when they have become overripe. This is the same method in which French Sauternes is made.

Grapes are allowed to enter a state called *Botrytis cinerea,* also known as noble rot. In this process the grapes are allowed to wither so that their natural juices and sugar become concentrated; simultaneously, natural acids are reduced. Making wines such as these is a risky and expensive process for vintners.

Reading a German Wine Label

A rating system categorizes German wines and this information is included on German wine labels. They range from least to most sweet.

• Kabinett:

Originally a term for wines locked in the cabinet, or cellar, today this term refers to wine made from fully mature grapes, without any sugar added. Kabinett wines are light and semi-dry (halb-trocken).

• Spätlese:

Late-picked grapes.

• Auslese:

Selected, or specially chosen, late-picked grapes.

• Beerenauslese:
   Fully ripened late-picked grapes.

• Trockenbeerenauslese:
   Raisined, fully ripened late-picked grapes.

• Eiswein:
   The ultimate sweet wine is called Eiswein, or ice-wine,
   which is made from grapes harvested and crushed after
   they have frozen on the vine. According to German law
   the grapes for Eiswein must be picked when the tem-

IS LESS BETTER?

In late 1991 major German wine producers introduced a smaller bottle size, shipping seven
white wines of the highly praised 1990 vintage to
the United States in 500-milliliter bottles. These
bottles hold four glasses of wine, in contrast to the
standard 750-milliliter bottle, which holds six. In
addition the alcoholic content of the wine ranges
from 8.5 to 11.5 percent, lower than the American
average of 12 percent.

German wine sales in the United States have
declined 75 percent since reaching an all-time
high in 1984. The plan to recapture the American
market involves appealing to Americans' health
concerns about moderate drinking.

The labels of these wines are also simplified
versions of the usually complicated Gothic ones:
they state the producer, the region in which the
grapes were grown, their level of ripeness and
sometimes the name of the grape. Some feel that
the 500-milliliter bottle will become increasingly
popular.

perature is between fourteen degrees above and eighteen degrees below zero.

HUNGARY

Hungary was one of the first countries to strictly regulate its wine industry according to place-name and grape variety. While its wines carry names that are difficult for most of us to pronounce, once you get beyond the unfamiliar spelling, you will find a variety of well-made and moderately priced wines.

Tokay: The Most Famous Hungarian Wine

Tokay (also known as Tokaj or Tokaji) is a sweet golden wine, renowned in Europe from the time of the Crusades. It is a late-gathered, dried-berry wine, similar to the French Sauternes and the German Trockenbeerenauslese. Sweet wines like these are made from overripe grapes harvested late in the season. Natural acids are reduced and sugar and juices become concentrated, as grapes wither into berry form and enter into a state of *Botrytis cinerea,* or noble rot.

Other Hungarian Wines

The most famous red wine of Hungary is Eger Bikavér, or "Bull's Blood," which is smooth, full-bodied and deeply colored. Its name comes from the sixteenth century, when local Hungarian soldiers were well fortified by the wine in a fight against Turkish forces. Hungarian white wines to look for include Badascony Szürkebarát, Debro Hárslevelü and Leányka.

ITALY

Italy produces and exports more wine than any other country in the world. And Italians drink more wine than anyone else—

including the French. Red wines are the favorite of Italians, and not surprisingly Italy's finest wines are red.

Red Wines

Italy produces some of the best red wines in the world. Types of Italian red wine include:

- Barbaresco:
  The lighter, somewhat underrated cousin of Barolo, Barbaresco often constitutes a better value for your dollar. Like Barolo it is rich, fragrant and dry, and benefits in flavor and bouquet through airing. Also made in Piedmont from the Nebbiolo grape.

- Barbera:
  The Barbera grape is usually linked on wine labels with district names such as d'Asti and di Cuneo. Barbera is the most common vine in Piedmont, and wines of widely varying quality are made from it. These wines share the robust and earthly flavor of wines made from the Nebbiolo grape, but are not as powerful or robust.

- Bardolino:
  Simple, fresh and clear red wine from Veneto. Slightly sweet, best drunk somewhat chilled and on the young side, when it is often slightly *frizzante* (Italian for semi-sparkling). Made from Molinara and Rondinella grapes.

- Barolo:
  Ruby red, powerful, robust and full-bodied. Considered by many wine critics to be the best wine of Italy. Barolos are aged a minimum of three years before they go on the market, and continue to improve with age. These wines are noted for their huge violet-scented bouquet. They should be allowed to air, or breathe, for as long as possible—at least three hours is recommended—before serving. Made in Piedmont from the Nebbiolo grape.

- Chianti:
  Chianti has shed the image of its old-fashioned wicker-covered bottles; today's Chiantis are sturdy and full-bodied. They are less tannic, or dry, than wines made from the Nebbiolo grape. Made in Tuscany from the Sangiovese grape.

- Dolcetto:
  A pleasantly rugged red wine in the style of Barbera. Light and drinkable, like a French Beaujolais. Dolcetto d'Alba is a popular variety of this Piedmont wine. Made from the Dolcetto grape.

- Gattinara:
  Preferred by some wine critics to Barolo, who consider Gattinara Italy's best wine. Less strong and more elegant than Barolo. Made in Piedmont from the Nebbiolo grape.

- Valpolicella:
  Simple, soft and fruity red wine from Veneto. Best drunk young, and slightly chilled. Made from Molinara and Corvina grapes.

- Vino Novello:
  Italy's answer to France's Beaujolais Nouveau. A dry red wine made by carbonic maceration; as in France, whole grapes are fermented under carbon dioxide in a tank. While the Gamay grape is used to make Beaujolais Nouveau, many different grapes are used in Vino Novello, including Barbera, Dolcetto and Nebbiolo. Best drunk slightly chilled, and may last longer than the two to six months usually estimated for Beaujolais Nouveau.

White Wines

Since the late 1960s—subsequent to Italy's enactment of laws controlling the quality of its wine—Italian white wines have experienced some major improvements. Types of Italian white wine include:

THE LEGEND OF EST! EST!! EST!!!

The story behind the name of Est! Est!! Est!!! is one of the great wine legends of Italy. In 1110 a bishop traveling from Augsburg to Rome sent his servant ahead of him with the instructions to write "Est!" on the door of any inn where the wine was good. When the servant reached the small town of Montefiasco, the wine was so good that in his enthusiasm he wrote Est! Est!! Est!!! on the door.

The good bishop never made it to Rome. He and his servant stayed in Montefiasco, drinking Est! Est!! Est!!! until the bishop drank himself into his grave. In his will he left everything to the small town, with one condition: each year, on the anniversary of his death, a barrel of Est! Est!! Est!!! should be poured over his grave.

- Est! Est! Est!!!:
   Dry with a hint of sweetness. Est! Est!! Est!!! is made in the Castelli Romani (Castles of Rome) district of Lazio.

- Frascati:
   Fragrant, medium-bodied, dry with a hint of sweetness. Known for its clear, golden color. The Frascati of Fontana Candida is widely available in the United States. Made from Trebbiano and Malvasia grapes in the Castelli Romani (Castles of Rome) district of Lazio.

- Orvieto:
   A medium-bodied dry wine. Made from the Trebbiano grape in Umbria.

- Pinot Grigio:
   A simple full-bodied wine, ranging in color from pale straw to copper. Made from the Pinot Gris grape in the Trentino–Alto Adige region.

• Soave:
   One of the most well-known white wines of Italy. Simple, dry and crisp. A firm, well-balanced wine, with a
   hint of floweriness in its bouquet. Made from Garganega
   and Trebbiano grapes in Veneto.

Italian Wine Regions and Producers

Piedmont, home of the Barolos and Barbarescos, is the premier wine-producing region of Italy. Tuscany and Veneto are
also major wine regions, and vines are grown and wine is made
throughout Italy.

Major Italian wine producers include Abbazzia dell' An-
nunciata, Antinori, Bersano, Bertani, Bertolli, Bolla, Cella,
Giuseppe Colla, Paolo Cordero, Folonari, Fontana Candida,
Marchesi De' Frescobaldi, Angelo Gaja, Lamberti, Martini &
Rossi, Mirafiore, Opera Pia, Orfevi, Pio Cesare, Principe Pal-
lavicini, Prunotto, Renato Ratti, Ricasoli, Ruffino, Santa Sofia,
Villa Banfi and Conde Zandotti.

SPAIN

Spain has more acres planted with wine grapes than any other
country in Europe. Only Italy and France, graced with soils
more hospitable to the grape, produce more wine than Spain.
The Phoenicians are thought to have been the first to plant
vines in Spain, in about 1100 B.C.

Earlier in our own century the Spanish Civil War and World
War II led to neglect, and a parasitic disease called *Phylloxera*
claimed many of the vines. However, production has risen
steadily since the 1950s. The establishments of Spanish winemakers are known as bodegas.

A French Influence

In the 1870s the grape louse *Phylloxera* destroyed the vineyards of Bordeaux in France. The disease fortunately did not
spread across the Pyrenees into Spain, so many French wine-

makers moved their vineyards to Rioja in Spain. Today many wine critics detect the influence of Bordeaux in Spanish Riojas.

Red Wines

When one thinks of wine from Spain, it is usually red wine. And, indeed, Spanish red wines are superior to the country's white ones. Red wines from Rioja range from soft and fruity to deep and full-bodied.

A range of colors defines these wines: rosado (pinkish), clarete (light red), ojo de gallo (eye of the rooster—or somewhere between light red and deep red) and tinto (deep red).

Rioja wines are made from grapes native to Spain, primarily the Garnacha (related to the French Grenache of the Rhône Valley) and the Tempranillo.

The Two Types of Rioja

• Light-Bodied:
  Bottles marked simply as Rioja.

• Full-Bodied:
  Wine in bottles marked Rioja Riserva or Rioja Gran Riserva have been aged longer in the cask or bottle, resulting in a richer wine. Gran Riservas are aged at least seven years.

White Wines

Spanish white wines can be either *dulce* (sweet) or *seco* (dry). As in the case of red wines, they are made from grapes native to Spain, including the Calagrano, Garnacha, Malvasia and Viura. Some of the best white wines of Spain—dry and full-flavored—are made by the Marqués de Riscal in Rioja.

Wine Regions and Producers of Spain

The two most important table wine regions are Rioja and Penedès in northern Spain.

Although red, white and rosé wines are all made in Rioja,

red Riojas are considered the best table wines of Spain. The bodegas of the Marqués de Cáceres, the Marqués de Riscal and the Marqués de Murrieta, all of Rioja, are among the most renowned in the country.

Codorníu and Freixenet sparkling wines are made in Penedés. There, the Torres winery also produces an assortment of good red and white wines.

Other wine regions include Valencia, which is famous for making sweet wines from grapes such as the Muscatel. In La Mancha, the land of Don Quixote, a few winemakers still use traditional *tinajas,* huge terra-cotta jars, rather than modern oak casks or glass-lined vats. Valdepeñas is one of the best known red wines of this region. In the coastal area of Alicante wineries produce strong red wines, with an alcoholic content reaching as high as 17 percent.

Seven

Food and Wine:
What Goes with What?

The marriage of wine and food is considered one in which both parties benefit; wine and food are each enhanced when served with the other.

The rules governing what wine goes with what food have eased considerably in recent years. Wine today is largely a matter of individual taste and preference. For example, some people will only drink either white or red with whatever they are eating.

But while wine experts agree that we are long past the rule of white wine with chicken and fish and red wine with meat, they also note that many traditional guidelines still hold true. The rosé that is perfect for an afternoon picnic would be out of place at a formal dinner; likewise a fine red Bordeaux or Burgundy would be wasted if casually quaffed with a midday sandwich.

The Demystification of Wine

A new emphasis on personal preference has widened our vinous horizons. For example, while oysters have traditionally been paired with French Chablis and "marry" or combine very well with this fine white wine, they are now often served with Bordeaux, Champagne, Muscadet and Sauvignon Blanc.

And all taste good. This loosening of customary pairings of foods and wines is seen by many as a good step in the demystification of wine.

Matching Foods and Wines

What are the traditional rules that still hold true? In general the heavier the food, the heavier the wine you will want to drink with it. Steaks, roast beef, game and pasta in meat sauces call for sturdy red wines.

Dry white wines are light and delicate, and are best accompanied by lighter fare, such as fowl and veal. Light reds can also fill the bill here.

Sweet wines are best at the end of the meal; served earlier in the meal, they will destroy your appetite. Aromatic wines, such as Gewürztraminers and Rieslings, pair well with spicy foods. A chilled rosé will complement light fare and is perfect with cold meat served at a summer picnic.

There are enthusiasts who proclaim that there is no wrong time for Champagne; legend has it that true aficionados even brush their teeth with it. But most of us drink dry or brut Champagne as an aperitif, alone or with caviar, smoked fish and other hors d'oeuvres, and sweeter demi-sec Champagne with dessert.

Are There Foods Which Do Not Go Well with Wine?

The foods that do not mix well with wine are in the minority, but there are a few. Vinegar will kill the taste of any wine. Some citrus fruits, such as grapefruit, are also best eaten without wine. Likewise, very pungent fish, such as anchovies or kippers, do not harmonize with wine.

But most foods can be successfully matched with a wine. Even salty foods, such as caviar, can be paired with wine; Champagne or other sparkling wines are best. And other foods that you might not think appropriate to combine with wine, such as Chinese and Thai cuisine, are nicely complemented by spicy Alsace or German Kabinett Rieslings and Gewürztraminers.

Does How the Food Is Prepared Matter?

Most definitely yes. Versatile chicken and pasta dishes vary so widely that it is impossible to make a blanket statement about any one wine that goes with them. Simple chicken dishes, for example, will marry well with very different wines than chicken prepared in heavy cream sauces.

Is There a Proper Order in Which to Serve Wine with Food?

In the restaurant or at home, if you are having more than one wine with dinner, here are a few guidelines to follow:

• Lighter and more delicate white wines are best served before red.

• If you are serving more than one red wine, stick with wines of a similar character: for example two Oregon Pinot Noirs from different vineyards.

• Younger wines should be served first, leading up to more elegant and mature wines.

Wine and Seasons

Just as you prefer lighter food in the summer, lighter wines are more suitable when the temperature climbs. Lightly chilled whites and rosés are refreshing complements to tropical meals.

On a chilly winter night, when a steak or hearty stew seems just the thing, likewise a heartier red wine is in order.

Popular Food and Wine Myths: True or False?

• Drink white wines with all fish and poultry.
   False. Richly flavored fish, such as striped bass and red

snapper, are nicely complemented by light- to medium-bodied red wines. Turkey and capon are among the fowl that can be served with either red or white wine. And roast chicken can be enjoyed with a wide variety of reds.

- White wines should always be served chilled.
  False. Simple white wines should be chilled to about forty-five degrees, but more complex white wines lose their subtle flavor and aroma through over-chilling. They are best drunk only slightly chilled, at fifty to sixty degrees.

- Drink only red wines with red meats.
  In general this is true. However, veal can be served with either red or white wine.

- All red wines should be served at room temperature.
  False. Simple red wines are best served chilled, just like simple whites. It is complex red wines that should be served at room temperature, between sixty-five and seventy degrees.

- All rosés are sweet.
  False. French Tavel Rosé is dry, as is the popular new category of California blush wine, vin gris. Rosés are versatile wines that complement most foods.

- All Champagne is dry.
  False. Champagne and other sparkling wines range from brut, or dry, to demi-sec, which is slightly sweet. Brut Champagne is best served before a meal, alone or with hors d'oeuvres; demi-sec Champagne often accompanies dessert.

An A to Z Guide to Food and Wines

The following guidelines of what goes with what are a good jumping-off point into the pleasures of well-paired food and wine. Note that many wines overlap in categories: Cabernets range from medium to full-bodied, while Zinfandels can be either full-bodied or robust. As you begin to sample more

wines yourself, you will bring this experience to the dinner
table and be able to make choices that best suit your own taste.

Antipasto

Light-bodied reds, such as Barbera, Dolcetto and
Valpolicella.
Light-bodied whites, such as Frascati, Orvieto and Pinot
Grigio.

Artichokes

A crisp Sauvignon Blanc.

Asparagus

Off-dry or slightly sweet white wines nicely complement
simply prepared asparagus. These include Chenin Blanc and
Riesling.
Asparagus in a hollandaise sauce is better served with crisp
and acidic young whites, such as Fumé Blanc or Sauvignon
Blanc.

Barbecued Meats

Medium-bodied reds, such as Barbera, Bardolino, Cabernet/
Shiraz, Côtes-du-Rhône, Dolcetto and Valpolicella are usually
perfect. But if your specialty is turbo-powered barbecue sauce,
go for the even more robust reds, such as Shiraz or Zinfandel.

Beef, Roast or Grilled

Full-bodied reds, such as Cabernet Sauvignons from the
United States, Australia or South America. Pinot Noirs and
Merlots from Oregon and California. Also Barbaresco, Barolo,
Bordeaux (such as Pomerol and St.-Emilion), Hermitage, Shi-
raz and Zinfandel.

Bluefish

Light red wines such as Cru Beaujolais.

Bouillabaisse

A light red, such as Côtes-du-Rhône, or a lightly chilled Tavel Rosé.

Capon

Medium-bodied wines, such as white Saint-Véran or red Pomerol.

Carpaccio

Complementary Italian reds include Barbera and Chianti.

Casseroles

Barbera, Bonny Doon Le Cigare Volant, Dolcetto, Cabernet/ Shiraz, Cabernet Sauvignon, Châteauneuf-du-Pape, Joseph Phelps and other Rhône-style California wines.

Caviar

Champagne and other sparkling wines.

Cheeses

* Mild or Young (Gouda, Port Salut, Monterey Jack, etc.):
    Fruity reds, such as Beaujolais, Napa Gamay or young Pinot Noirs. Fruity whites, such as Riesling. German and Austrian Kabinett wines.

* Strong or Aged (Cheddar, Fontina, Parmesan, etc.):
    Full-bodied red wines, such as Cabernet/Shiraz, Cabernet Sauvignon, Châteauneuf-du-Pape, Côte Rôtie, Gattinara or Hermitage.

* Blue Cheese:
    Late harvest sweet wines, such as German Spätlese and Trockenbeerenauslese, or French Sauternes. Also look for late harvest wines from California.

• **Goat Cheese (Chèvre):**
  This is the best cheese to enjoy with full-bodied reds,
  such as Hill-Smith Shiraz, Oregon Pinot Noirs, Rhône
  reds and California Cabernet Sauvignon. In the white
  category, Sauvignon Blanc from producers such as Miguel Torres of Chile, crisp and herbaceous Sancerre, and
  dry but fruity Pinot Grigio combine well with goat
  cheese.

• **Double or Triple Crème Cheeses:**
  Creamy whites, such as Burgundy or Chardonnay. Also
  Champagne and other sparkling wines.

Chicken

• **Roast or Grilled Chicken:**
  Red wines: Barbaresco, Cru Beaujolais, Cabernet Sau-
  vignon, Chianti Riserva, Côtes-du-Rhône, Gattinara,
  Hermitage, Médoc, Pinot Noir, Rioja Riserva, Shiraz,
  Volnay and Zinfandel.
    White wines: Chardonnay, Sauvignon Blanc and
  German Kabinett wines.

• **Chicken Salad:**
  American, French or Chilean rosés, such as Simi, Tavel
  and Concha y Toro Merlot Blanc. Blush wines, including the Pinot Noir Blanc of Buena Vista or Monterey
  vineyards in California. Also a crisp and acidic Mâcon-
  Villages.

• **Fried Chicken:**
  Barbera, Beaujolais, Chianti, Dolcetto, Napa Gamay and
  Rioja (light style).

• **Chicken in a Cream Sauce:**
  A crisp Saint-Véran or an oaky Chardonnay.

Chili

A chilled rosé or Beaujolais.

Chinese Food

Spicy wines, such as Gewürztraminer and Riesling from Austria, France or the United States.

Chops

Thick chops are best complemented by wines such as an oaky and intense Zinfandel. Alexander Valley, for example, produces a full-bodied Zinfandel with a rich bouquet of berries and spice.

Clams

Steamed clams are nicely accompanied by a dry and zesty Pinot Grigio.

Cold Cuts

Beaujolais and other light and fruity red wines. In the white category, German and Austrian Kabinett wines. Also Tavel Rosé from France and American blush wines, such as the Pinot Noir Blanc of Buena Vista or Monterey vineyards in California.

Curry

Wines that are distinctive in taste, notably Gewürztraminer, Sancerre and Sauvignon Blanc.

Desserts

A sweet wine, such as Sauternes, Barsac or demi-sec Champagne.

Duck

An American Merlot or Pinot Noir.

Fish

• Grilled and Other Light Fish Dishes:
With simply grilled or steamed sole or trout, light red
wines, such as Beaujolais and Rioja (light style), are
appropriate accompaniments. So are a wide variety of
crisp young white wines, including Fumé Blanc, Muscadet, Orvieto, Pinot Grigio, Saint-Véran, Sancerre, Los
Vascos Sauvignon Blanc, Soave and Torres Viña Sol.

• Full-Flavored Fish:
Fish such as striped bass and red snapper are nicely
joined with full-bodied whites, such as oaky Chardonnays and French Burgundies.

• Meatier Fish:
Cru Beaujolais, Merlot and Pinot Noir are a good match
for meaty salmon, swordfish and tuna.

• Fish in White or Butter Sauce:
Full-bodied whites, such as Chardonnay and white Bur-
gundy (Mâcon-Villages, Corton-Charlemagne, Puligny-
Montrachet, etc.).

Foie Gras

Semi-dry or sweet wines: Barsac, Gewürztraminer, Sauternes, Vouvray.

Frankfurters

Beaujolais Nouveau or Vino Novello.

Fruit

Semi-dry white wines, such as demi-sec Champagne,
Chenin Blanc, Gewürztraminer, Riesling and Vouvray.

Game

Robust reds to match their strong flavors, such as Barolo, Barbaresco, Brunello, Cabernet Sauvignon, Chianti Riserva, Crozes-Hermitage, Pinot Noir, Côte Rôtie, Syrah and Zinfandel.

Grilled Red Meats

Fruity young reds, such as Barbera, Bardolino, Cabernet/ Shiraz, Côte de Brouilly, Eger Bikavér, Sangre de Toro, South American Cabernets and Zinfandel.

Ham

Light reds or rosés, such as Beaujolais or Tavel Rosé. Blush wines, including the Pinot Noir Blanc of Buena Vista or Monterey vineyards in California. Also Chardonnay.

Hamburgers

Beaujolais-Villages, Chianti, Côtes-du-Rhône, Napa Gamay, Navarro Correas Syrah, Pinot Blanc, Sangre de Toro, Zinfandel.

Indian Food

A semi-dry wine, such as Alsace Gewürztraminer. A light and fruity chilled Beaujolais will nicely offset very hot dishes.

Italian Sausage

Lusty reds, including Barolo and Zinfandel.

Japanese Food

Light dry white wines, such as Macôn-Villages.

Lamb

Full-bodied reds: Cabernet Sauvignon, Merlot, Rioja (full-bodied), Zinfandel.

Lasagna

Barbaresco, Barbera, Barolo and other medium- to full-bodied reds.

Liver

A dry Vouvray from France's Loire Valley, or a fruity Beaujolais from Burgundy.

Lobster

Champagne or other sparkling wine. California Chardonnays, white French Burgundy, Bordeaux or Chablis. German or Austrian Kabinett wines.

Mexican Food

Blush wines, such as Pinot Noir Blanc or white Zinfandel. Rosés, such as Mirassou Petite Rosé or Robert Mondavi Woodbridge Gamay Rosé.

Middle Eastern Food

Rosés with couscous and chicken dishes. Light reds, such as Rhônes and Riojas with meats. Australian Shiraz or full-bodied Californian Cabernets with shish kebab.

Oysters

Chablis, Champagne and other sparkling wines. Fumé Blanc, Muscadet, Sémillon, white Bordeaux.

Paella

A classic Spanish dish well matched with red or white Riojas.

Pasta

• Primavera:
    Light and fruity young wines, such as red Beaujolais, white Gavi di Gavi, Soave or Torres Viña Sol.

• In a Hearty Tomato Sauce, Such As Bolognese or Putanesca:
    Barbera, Bardolino, Chianti, Dolcetta, Valpolicella.

• With Shellfish:
    In the red category, a light-bodied Cabernet Sauvignon or Merlot. Also white wines, including Muscadet, Pinot Grigio, Sancerre and Sauvignon Blanc.

• In a Cream Sauce, Such As Alfredo:
    Chardonnay, Soave.

• With Garlic or Pesto:
    Chardonnay, Pinot Grigio.

Pâté

Semi-dry or sweet white wines, such as Barsac, Gewürztraminer, Pinot Blanc, Sauternes, Vouvray. Also a herbaceous Sancerre. In the red category, light and fruity young Pinot Noirs, slightly chilled.

Picnics

Light chilled wines, including Beaujolais, Grenache Rosé, Robert Mondavi Woodbridge Gamay Rosé, Simi Rosé, Tavel Rosé and white Zinfandel.

Pizza

Barbaresco, Bardolino, Barolo, Beaujolais, Brouilly, Chianti, Chiroubles, Egri Bikaver and other light- to medium-bodied reds.

Pork, Roast

Pinot Noir and Rioja (full-bodied) are good complements to roast pork.

Pork Chops

Red Concha y Toro Merlot or white Navarro Correas Chardonnay both marry well with pork chops.

Prime Rib

Prime rib calls for good, strong, stick-to-your-ribs type wines, such as Cabernet Sauvignon, Châteauneuf-du-Pape, Chianti, Rioja (full-bodied) and Shiraz.

Prosciutto

Complementary Italian reds include Barolo and Chianti.

Quiche

A Côtes-du-Rhône or Cru Beaujolais will go well with quiche, as will crisp and acidic Mâcon-Lugny and Mâcon-Villages.

Red Snapper

Full-bodied whites, such as Chardonnay and white Burgundy (Mâcon-Villages, Corton-Charlemagne, Puligny-Montrachet, etc.).

Roasted Meats

Barolo, Cabernet Sauvignon, Shiraz, Zinfandel and other hearty reds.

Salade Niçoise

A lightly chilled rosé, such as Simi or Robert Mondavi Woodbridge.

Salads

A salad with an intense vinegar-based dressing is best served without wine; the vinegar makes the wine taste flat.

With fruit or herb dressing, however, a highly acidic wine will balance the flavors. Examples include Fumé Blanc, Orvieto, Sancerre and Sauvignon Blanc.

Salmon

A medium-bodied red Graves, Merlot or Pinot Noir—or a white Chardonnay—are among the wines that can nicely accompany grilled salmon. Sauvignon Blanc is a better choice when salmon is prepared in a mustard or green sauce.

Sausages

Côtes-du-Rhône, Navarro Correas Syrah, Sangre de Toro and Sangria.

Seafood

Simply prepared seafood is best complemented by crisp, light, acidic white wines, such as Fumé Blanc, Muscadet, Saint-Véran, Sancerre, Sauvignon Blanc and Soave.

Shish Kebab

Sturdy reds, such as Australian Cabernet/Shiraz or full-bodied California Cabernets.

Shrimp

- Boiled:
  Macôn-Villages or an American Chardonnay.

- Grilled:
  Fumé Blanc, Sauvignon Blanc, Viña Sol of Miguel Torres.

- Scampi:
  To best meet the strong and garlicky flavor, try a Chardonnay or French Chablis.

Smoked Fish (Salmon, Bluefish, Trout, etc.)

Champagne and other sparkling wines, German Kabinett Rieslings, Gewürztraminer, Sancerre, Sauvignon Blanc, Tokay, Vouvray.

Soft-Shell Crabs

Medium-bodied whites, including Pouilly-Fumé, Pouilly-Fuissé, and Saint-Véran.

Sole

Simply prepared sole is best accompanied by delicate white wines, including Macôn-Villages and Saint-Véran. When sole is prepared in a cream sauce, a richer wine is desirable, such as Puligny-Montrachet or California Chardonnay.

Soup

Good company to hearty soups is provided by medium-bodied red wines, such as Barbera, Bonny Doon Le Cigare Volant, Dolcetto, Cabernet/Shiraz, Cabernet Sauvignon, Châteauneuf-du-Pape and Rhône-style California wines.

With lighter soups, such as French onion soup or Vichyssoise, try a light white wine, such as Pinot Blanc or Entre-Deux-Mers.

Spicy Foods

Marry well with spicy wines, such as Gewürztraminer.

Steak

Full-bodied reds, such as Cabernet Sauvignon, Châteauneuf-du-Pape, Chianti, Merlot, Rioja (full-bodied), Shiraz and Zinfandel.

Stew

The hearty flavor of stew pairs well with full-bodied reds, such as Barbera, Bonny Doon Le Cigare Volant, Dolcetto, Cabernet/Shiraz, Cabernet Sauvignon and Châteauneuf-du-Pape.

Striped Bass

Full-bodied whites, such as Chardonnay and white Burgundy (Corton-Charlemagne, Puligny-Montrachet, etc.).

Sushi

Champagne and other sparkling wines.

Sweetbreads

Fruity young red wines, such as Beaujolais and Côtes-du-Rhône.

Swordfish

Medium-bodied red wines, such as Merlot and Pinot Noir. Also herbaceous Sauvignon Blanc.

Tarts

Dessert tarts are best accompanied by a sweet wine, such as Sauternes or Barsac.

Tex-Mex

California rosés, such as Grenache, Mirassou, Robert Mondavi or Simi.

Thai Food

For lightly sauced dishes, a Pinot Grigio or Sancerre. Spicy dishes call for a blush wine, such as white Zinfandel. Try a Merlot with red meats.

Trout

Light white wines, such as Muscadet, Orvieto, Pinot Grigio, Soave and Verdicchio.

Tuna

- Grilled Tuna:
  Medium-bodied reds, such as Beaune, Gattinara, Merlot or Pinot Noir.

- Tuna Fish Salad:
  Dry vin gris or a light and fruity white.

Turkey

A traditional Thanksgiving dinner is well complemented by zesty American Zinfandels, from producers such as Alexander Valley, Clos du Val, Fetzer, Grgich Hills, Ravenswood, Ridge Vineyards, Storybook Mountain and Sutter Home.

Veal

- Chops or Scallopini:
  Medium-bodied red wines, such as Bordeaux, Cabernet Sauvignon, Merlot and Pinot Noir. Also strong young Beaujolais.

• In a Cream Sauce:
    Rich and creamy whites, such as a French Burgundy or
    an oaky California Chardonnay.

• Piccata:
    A Sauvignon Blanc to counter the lemony flavor.

Venison

Robust red wines, such as Barolo, Châteauneuf-du-Pape,
Hermitage, Petite Sirah, Shiraz, Syrah and Zinfandel.

Vietnamese Food

Spicy wines to meet the assertive flavor of assertive Viet-
namese dishes include Alsace Gewürztraminers. A dry rosé or
sparkling wine would also be appropriate.

Eight

Different Grapes for Different Groups: Entertaining with Wine

Entertaining with wine is a rewarding experience, whether you are serving an elegant dinner to a small number of guests or having an open house. But what style of wine should you serve? How much wine should you buy for each occasion? Is there a way to stretch your wine—and your wine dollars? And how should wine be served?

Styles and Amounts of Wine to Serve

The style and amount of wine you serve depends on the group you are entertaining and the occasion for which you have invited them. Here are some guidelines that can help.

At a Brunch

Champagne and other sparkling wines make any brunch into a special occasion. Accompany your brunch with sparkling wine alone or try one of the following delicious concoctions. In both cases the wine should be chilled first, in the refrigerator or ice bucket.

Keep in mind that mixed drinks are also festive and more economical than sparkling wine served alone. In addition, lower-priced sparkling wines are appropriate to use when you intend to mix them; better sparkling wines should be savored on their own. Always remember to stir Champagne cocktails very gently so as not to destroy the bubbles in them. Following are the recipes for a few favorite sparkling wine cocktails:

- Bellini:
  Puree one fresh ripe peach and pour into the bottom of a tall, chilled wineglass (8 to 10 ounces.) Add sparkling wine.

- Champagne Cocktail:
  Place a sugar cube, a twist of lemon and a dash of bitters in a tall, chilled wineglass. Add sparkling wine.

- Mimosa:
  Mix equal parts of orange juice and sparkling wine in a tall, chilled wineglass.

- Kir Royale:
  Fill three-quarters of a tall, chilled wineglass with sparkling wine. Top off with a few drops of crème de cassis (black currant liqueur) and garnish with a lemon peel. (For a simple Kir, substitute sparkling wine with still white wine.)

At a Dinner Party

The style of wine you choose to accompany your dinner is the one that best complements the food you are serving. As mentioned earlier, lighter meals call for lighter wines, while heavier dishes demand heavier, more full-bodied wines. Consult Chapter Seven, ''Food and Wine,'' for some specific suggestions.

Before dinner, as an aperitif, or stimulant to the appetite, you might offer your guests a glass of sparkling wine or a wine cocktail.

After the meal, either alone or with dessert, you might choose a sweeter wine, such as a French Sauternes, or a late harvest wine from Germany, Alsace or California.

For a formal dinner party, count on serving each guest an average of four glasses of wine: one before dinner, two during dinner and one after dinner.

For a dinner party of six, this would translate into

• One bottle of sparkling wine.
• Two bottles of the wine or wines you wish to serve with dinner.
• One bottle of dessert wine.

WINE COCKTAILS

As an aperitif before a dinner party, many hosts serve wine cocktails such as the following:

• Cardinal:
  Fill three-quarters of a tall wineglass with chilled Beaujolais. Top off with a few drops of crème de cassis (black currant liqueur) and garnish with a lemon peel.

• Kir:
  Fill three-quarters of a tall wineglass with chilled white wine. Top off with a few drops of crème de cassis (black currant liqueur) and garnish with a lemon peel.

• Spritzer:
  Put three or four ice cubes into a balloon-shaped wineglass. Add four ounces of white or red wine and two ounces of club soda, and garnish with a lemon or lime wedge.

At an Open House

An open house or drop-in poses an entirely different set of wine considerations. To calculate how much wine to buy, count on your guests drinking at the rate of two drinks per person per hour.

In a party of ten or more there are bound to be both red and white wine drinkers, so more variety is needed in the wine you purchase. Jug wines are the perfect answer when you are entertaining a large group of people like this. While a normal

JUG WINES

- Almaden
- Barbella
- Boucheron
- Concha y Toro
- Georges Duboeuf
- Fetzer
- Folonari
- Fontana Candida
- Gallo
- Glen Ellen
- Inglenook
- Los Vascos
- Paul Masson
- Mirassou
- Robert Mondavi Woodbridge
- Monterey
- J. Moreau
- Raymond Pedroncelli
- Partager
- Principato
- Carlo Rossi
- Round Hill
- Sebastiani
- Seghesio
- Taylor
- M.G. Vallejo

bottle of wine is 750 milliliters (25.4 ounces) and holds six glasses of wine, jugs may range from 1.5 liters to 4 liters—or twelve to thirty-two glasses.

How to Stretch the Wine for a Big Party

Mixing wine with spices, fruit juices or club soda is a cheerful way of entertaining your guests. It can dress up an average wine and also make the amount of wine you serve go farther.

Serving punch at a large gathering can be a festive and economical alternative. And once you have made it, you can relax and enjoy the party with your guests, who are free to serve themselves. It's helpful, however, to keep an extra bowl of the mixture in your refrigerator, in case you run out.

Pat's Champagne Punch

(About 18 servings)
My sister Pat has been serving this delicious punch at parties for twenty years. Here's a happy way to brighten any holiday occasion.

* Thaw two 9-ounce packages of frozen strawberries.
* Combine the two thawed packages of frozen strawberries with twelve ounces of club soda or ginger ale.
* Place a block of ice in the bottom of a punch bowl.
Or, for a more festive touch, instead freeze ice in a circular mold and use that to keep your punch chilled. If you want to get very fancy—as my sister often does—freeze edible flowers or juice in an ice-cube tray and float them in your punch.
* Pour the strawberry mixture into the punch bowl.
* Add one quart of softened raspberry or orange sherbet in scoops.
* Add two 750-milliliter bottles of a low-priced sparkling wine such as André and mix gently.
* Garnish cups of punch with fresh strawberries. A sprig of fresh mint is a nice optional touch.

Cranberry Punch

(About 16 servings)
A delicious concoction to warm your friends on those cold winter nights, especially around the holidays.

* Heat two cans of frozen cranberry juice concentrate and 2½ cups of water in a large pot.
* Add one fresh orange studded with cloves.
* Add three sticks of cinnamon and eight opened cardamom pods.
* Stir in a 750-milliliter bottle of a simple red wine.
* If desired, add sugar or honey to taste.
* Serve warm, with cinnamon sticks as a garnish.

Mulled Wine

(About 12 servings)
Another warm and spicy favorite to drink when you're curled up round the fire.

* Pour a 1.5-liter bottle of red jug wine into a large pot.
* Add one fresh orange studded with cloves.

WINE PARTY PARAPHERNALIA

Here's a quick checklist of items to have on hand for your party:
* Ice
* Club Soda
* Fruit Juice
* Ice Bucket(s)
* Corkscrew
* Glasses
* Swizzle Sticks
* Cocktail Napkins

• Add two sticks of cinnamon, ¼ teaspoon allspice and ¼ teaspoon nutmeg.
• Simmer fifteen to twenty minutes, stirring occasionally, to allow the spices to flavor the wine.
• If desired, add sugar to taste.
• Serve warm, with cinnamon sticks as a garnish.

Sangría

(About 16 servings)
If your party theme is Mexican or Tex-Mex, Sangría is the perfect accompaniment to salsa and chips.

• Pour several trayfuls of ice into the bottom of a punch bowl.
• Pour a 1.5-liter bottle of red jug wine over the ice cubes.
• Stir in a sixteen-ounce bottle of club soda.
• Garnish with a combination of orange, lemon and lime slices. Chunks of pineapple are optional.

Talk to Your Wine Merchant

Now that you have an idea of the style and amount of wine you want, it's time to visit your favorite wine store. Talk to the wine merchant. You can discuss the choices you have made—and perhaps the wine merchant will have some suggestions of his or her own to add. For example, the merchant may be featuring some specials, or wines on sale, that fit into your game plan.

In many states it is legal to return unused bottles of wine. Talk to your local wine merchant to find out what the laws concerning this practice are in your state, and also his or her policy on unused bottles; when you are buying in quantity for a large party, there's always a plus or minus factor of a bottle or two. Many wine merchants, when approached in advance, will accept back unused bottles.

How to Serve Wine

At What Temperature Should Wine Be Served?

Different wines are at their best at different temperatures. As a general rule, the better the wine, the less you should chill it; chilling dulls a wine's flavor and aroma.

The following guidelines can be even better followed if you purchase a handy little device called a wine thermometer. They are available in most shops that sell wine implements. Simply insert the thermometer into the opened bottle that you plan to serve—the top of the thermometer is wider so it won't slip into the bottle—and you can determine if your wine has reached its optimal serving temperature.

- White Wines:
  Simple white wines can be chilled thoroughly, to approximately forty-five degrees. More complex white wines will lose their subtle bouquet and flavor through over-chilling. They are best drunk only slightly chilled, at fifty to sixty degrees.

- Red Wines:
  Simple red wines, such as Valpolicella and Bardolino, are best served chilled like simple whites. Young and fruity Beaujolais is also meant to be chilled.
  Complex red wines should be served at room temperature, approximately sixty-five to seventy degrees.

- Rosé Wines:
  Chill thoroughly, to approximately forty-five degrees.

- Sparkling Wines:
  Simple sparkling wines can be chilled to forty-five degrees; more complex ones will retain their flavor and aroma if less thoroughly chilled.

What Are the Most Efficient Methods of Chilling Wine?

In chilling wines you basically have two options: either refrigerate it or plunge it into ice water.

• Refrigerating Wine:

   Refrigerate wine two hours before serving. A refrigerator should not, by the way, be used to store wines for long periods of time; prolonged refrigeration will dull a wine's flavor and bouquet.

• Plunging Wine into Ice Water:

   This is the most efficient way of chilling wine. Submerge the wine totally for twenty minutes.

YOUR BATHTUB IS A GIANT ICE BUCKET

On my daughter Caitlin's first birthday, we ran out of ice buckets and refrigerator room for the Taittinger Comte de Comtes. So we simply put the bottles in the bathtub with several bags of ice and covered them with cold water. Caitlin's birthday toast was just as successful with Champagne chilled in the bathtub!

How to Prepare Wine in Advance for a Party

In Chapter Three you read about the pluses and minuses of letting wines breathe or decanting them before serving. If you are serving a wine which you believe will benefit by breathing, make sure that your party schedule includes time to accomplish this.

The wines that can profit from this process are usually young and tannic reds, which become gradually smoother when exposed to the air. Robust red wines also need time to soften.

Decanting a wine, as mentioned earlier, means pouring it into a glass or decanter in order to allow it to breathe. Decanting is also appropriate for some older red wines, which may contain sediment.

If You're Serving Sparkling Wine

Events such as New Year's Eve parties and weddings seem to call for extra festive wine, and Champagne is always a popular choice. But remember that popping the cork and letting it fly is not the best way to open a bottle of sparkling wine; a flying cork might hit someone, and in opening a bottle in this fashion you also squander your bubbles.

For the proper way to open a bottle of Champagne or other sparkling wine, refer back to the instructions in Chapter Three. To recap briefly, slant the bottle away from people, grasp the cork firmly, and twist the bottle in one direction to slowly remove the cork.

The Proper Wineglass

Remember that the size, shape and color of wineglasses all contribute to the wine's taste and presentation. A ten- to twelve-ounce glass that tapers in at the top is best for appreciating the aroma and flavor of wine. Wineglasses should also be clear, so that you can appreciate the color of a wine. For more detailed information on wineglasses, refer to the section concerning them in Chapter Three.

Other Glassware Considerations

The type of glasses in which you serve wine depends on the style of your party and what glasses you already have on hand.

For a large open house, take an inventory of your glasses. How many people have you invited and how many glasses do

THE SIZES OF CHAMPAGNE BOTTLES

- Split: ¼ bottle
- Half Bottle: ½ bottle
- Bottle
- Magnum: 2 bottles
- Jeroboam: 4 bottles
- Methuselah: 8 bottles
- Salmanazar: 12 bottles
- Balthazar: 16 bottles
- Nebuchadnezzar: 20 bottles

you have? Will everyone be drinking wine at once? You might have either to replace or supplement your own glasses with plastic ones from the store—although the wine will lose something in the process. Also consider borrowing extra glasses from a neighbor.

If you're having a very large open house, as contrasted to a small dinner party, you might want to think twice before serving wine in your best crystal. People bump into each other and accidents do happen.

Nine

Best Cellars:
How to Store Wine

The notion of a wine cellar conjures up images of another era, when hosts would descend into labyrinthine cellars and emerge with ancient, cobweb-covered bottles of wine.

Cellars today are quite a different matter. Modern storage facilities range from racks tucked away into corners of city apartments to closets set aside for wine storage in suburban homes.

What Is the Ideal Wine Cellar?

The ideal wine cellar is spacious, roomy, airy and not excessively dry. It has plenty of ventilation, so that the air doesn't get musty or too humid. The temperature is between fifty-three and fifty-seven degrees, and the humidity level is 60 to 70 percent. It is free from light and vibration.

The Bottom Line in Cellars

Whatever the nature of your living arrangements, the storage of wine calls for certain basic conditions. In order to successfully begin your new wine cellar, you must deal with the issues of:

- Space
- Temperature
- Humidity
- Light
- Vibration

Space

A well-ventilated space is the first necessity for your wine storage.

Proper ventilation is necessary to ensure the air doesn't become stale and musty. A musty atmosphere could permeate corks over time, possibly imparting a moldy taste to the wine.

Because today's cellars are often not the ideal location—in fact, many of us today don't even have cellars—it's necessary to be a little bit creative.

Think about corners and closets; adding some insulation to a closet near an outside wall will make a fine modern wine "cellar." But more on space and storage capacity a little later.

Temperature

The best wine storage area has a temperature which has two leading characteristics:

- The temperature is cool.

- The temperature is stable.

There are a number of considerations to keep in mind regarding the proper temperature for storing wine:

- A constant temperature of approximately fifty-three to fifty-seven degrees is the ideal environment for wine.

- The easiest way to monitor the temperature of the area where you store your wine is to purchase a thermometer and install it there. If you find that the temperature is too warm or too variable, you can search for a better storage area.

WINE AND THE REFRIGERATOR

It's not a good idea to store wine in the refrigerator for an indefinite period, since it may affect the aroma and flavor of a wine.

If, however, you open a bottle of wine which you do not finish, it is a good idea to refrigerate it. Most opened bottles—unless they are very old— will last three or four days in the refrigerator. For still wines, simply reinsert the cork. A special inexpensive corklike device is sold in wine stores to reseal Champagne and other sparkling wines.

• White wines and fragile older wines are more susceptible to heat than red ones. These should be stored in the coolest and most stable area of your facility; closest to the floor is best.

• Wines can adapt to gradually rising temperatures; it is a swift change in temperature that will damage them.

• The worst place to store wine: near a furnace or hot pipes.

• The best place to store wine: an area where the constant temperature is cooler than normal room temperature, such as the basement, a closet or near an outside wall.

Humidity

A constant humidity level between 60 and 70 percent is the ideal environment for storing wine. A certain amount of humidity is a good thing; it prevents corks from drying out prematurely.

But too much humidity will cause labels to mold, and while this will not damage the wine inside the bottle, the label on the bottle may rot away. The famous English wine authority Hugh Johnson recommends a quick squirt of hairspray over the label to prevent this from happening.

DOES THE COLOR OF THE
WINE BOTTLE MATTER?

Yes. Most wine bottles are dark green or brown in order to protect the wine within from light. Wine in clear bottles is especially vulnerable to damage by light.

If, on the other hand, there is not sufficient humidity, a cork may dry up prematurely and cause the wine in the bottle to oxidize or maderize. Under improper storage conditions, wines—especially whites and fragile older wines—can age prematurely, making them taste flat and turn brownish in color, like Madeira. While maderization adds to the greatness of the fortified Madeira wines of Portugal, in other white wines it is a defect.

If your storage area is not sufficiently humid, put a humidifier in the area. If you don't have one, a bowl of wet sand will do the trick.

Light

Wine cannot be stored in direct sun or artificial light. Strong light of any kind can oxidize or maderize your wine; that is, it can age wines—especially white wines—prematurely, making them taste flat and turn brownish in color.

Vibration

Wine cannot be stored next to the dishwasher—or washing machine or dryer—or any household appliance that causes excessive vibration. By the same token if you live very close to a railroad, take care that your wine is not stored in the part of the house that vibrates the most when trains go by.

Vibration, like excessive light, can cause wine to oxidize or maderize—that is, it can age prematurely, turning flat, brownish in color and musty.

TODAY'S CELLARS AND WINE STORAGE

The cellars of yesteryear were spacious, cool, humid, dark and quiet—in short, ideal places to store your wine. Today's cellars—with furnaces, washing machines and dryers, playrooms, etc.—may actually be the least desirable space to stow your wine!

In What Position Should Wines Be Stored?

Wines should be stored on their sides. This is so the wine will continue to touch and wet the cork. A dried-out cork causes the wine to oxidize, or become dull and flat. White wine is especially susceptible to this problem.

What Is the Advantage of Storing Wines?

American wine consumption has almost doubled since 1960. And as more people in the 1990s turn from going out to dinner to dining with family and friends at home, it's both handy and economical to keep wine at hand in your home rather than run out for a bottle on each occasion.

• Buying in advance gives you time to consider which wines you would most prefer to collect. Storing wines in your home allows you to purchase the wines you want, rather than run out at the last minute and settle for whatever is available.

• Storing wines also allows you to take advantage of sales in wine stores.

• When you buy wines by the case, you may get as much as a 10 percent discount.

• If you want to experiment with fine wines, your best bet is to buy them when they are young—and cheaper—and allow them to age in your home.

What Is Your Storage Capacity?

In today's modern apartments and homes, time and consideration is necessary to find the space best suited to successfully store wine.

An attractive wine rack, for example, can nicely accent a nonworking fireplace. An extra space at the bottom of a linen closet can accommodate a bin, cube or cabinet. For a temperature-controlled unit, you need extra space in a spare room or basement.

There are dozens of wine storage units available; a little shopping around and you will find the one that is right for you.

Wine Racks

Investing in an economical wooden or metal wine rack is a good place to begin your wine collection. Wine racks are a neat way to store your wine; you can properly store the bottles on their sides, and they are readily accessible.

There are stackable rack kits and modular wine racks that let you meet your present needs and allow room for future expansion. They assemble easily from floor to ceiling.

Bins, Cubes and Cabinets

Bins are spacious, jumbo containers that can hold up to 120 bottles each. If your plan for a wine cellar is an ambitious one, bins offer exceptional value for your money.

Cubes are an attractive and effective way in which to store cases of wine. They are also stackable and hold up to eighty bottles in 4 twenty-bottle compartments.

Cabinets, unlike most bins and cubes, have backings. They are stackable and hold up to sixty-four bottles each.

Temperature-Controlled Units

For the wine enthusiast who wants to invest in a sophisticated storage system, temperature-controlled units begin at around seven hundred dollars and climb steadily up from there. They look a little like the old-fashioned wardrobes that preceded modern closets. Smaller cabinets store fifty bottles in a temperature- and humidity-controlled environment; modular wine rooms hold up to three thousand bottles!

The Diversified Wine Cellar

The best cellars have a balanced selection, with a variety of wines from which to choose. However, the styles of wine should reflect those that you personally prefer and those that best complement the foods you ordinarily serve to your family and guests.

Styles of Wine

The styles of wine with which you stock your cellar are largely a matter of personal preference. Americans drink far more white wine than red; in fact, red wine accounts for only about 20 percent of wine sold in the United States. If you, too, are more likely to ask for a glass of white than red, then the wines you choose to store should reflect this preference.

In choosing wines for your collection, you should also consider the types of food you most often eat. Do you lean more toward lighter or heavier foods? Remember that lighter foods are best accompanied by light-bodied wines—whether white, rosé or red—while heavier meals, especially red meat, are better complemented by more full-bodied red wines.

Foreign or Domestic?

About three-quarters of the wine drunk in the United States is domestic. By all means "Buy American," and support domestic winemakers, who produce good wines at economical prices.

But much of the pleasure we get in drinking wines is through exploration and experimentation. Don't neglect to check out the wonderful wines all around the globe. As you can see in the Index of Common, Economical and Tasteful

Wines, good wines under ten dollars are available from countries throughout the world.

Do Vintages Matter?

The vintage, or year in which a wine is made, is always a matter of significance. Certain wines are better drunk young, while others need time to mature.

In addition, the weather conditions in different parts of the world determine the quality of vintages for fine wines. Some of the best recent vintages of French wines are noted in Chapter Five, "The Wines of France." For more detailed information on vintages, refer to a recent vintage chart or discuss the matter with your wine merchant.

Are There Wines That Do Not Benefit From Storage?

Emphatically yes. Beaujolais Nouveau from France and Vino Novello from Italy should be drunk soon after they are made—within three to six months.

Jug wines are also best consumed when they are young and fresh. Far from benefiting through age, they lose the youthful zing that makes them refreshing.

As a general rule, simple everyday wines are meant to be drunk within six months to a year of purchase. It's good to keep these wines on hand in your storage area, but you should note in your cellar book when you purchase them—do not allow too much time to go by before opening them. Drink them when they are young and at their best.

Keeping a Cellar Book

In order to keep track of the wines in your cellar, it is useful and convenient to begin a cellar record book. Some of the first printed cellar books were kept by English wine connoisseurs in the 1700s.

Cellar books are on sale in stores specializing in wine paraphernalia, but a spiral notebook will also do the trick. It's best to leave a full page for each wine. What information do you want to include in your cellar book?

• The full name of the wine, with other pertinent information, such as its year, producer and shipper.

• Where you purchased the wine.

• How much you paid for it.

• When it should be drunk—is it an everyday wine best drunk soon, or is it a fine wine that will benefit by aging?

• After entering the initial data, leave room to record the following: when and where you drank the wine, the company you shared, what food you ate with it, and—most important of all—your impressions, or tasting notes, of the wine.

• Many people also enjoy collecting wine labels. They steam them off the bottles and paste them on the appropriate page of their wine cellar book.

Bottle Tags: A Good Way to Keep Track of Your Wines

Tagging each bottle is a handy way to organize your collection attractively and efficiently, allowing you to choose the wine you want at a glance without disturbing your other bottles. You can make your own tags or buy them at a wine store.

Tie a tag onto the neck of a bottle with a piece of string. On the tag, write when and where you bought the wine, its price, and when it will be mature for drinking.

Sample Wine Cellars

If you have now come to the conclusion that you would like to have your own wine cellar, where do you begin in stocking it?

Let's return to our basic premise that the best cellar offers balance and variety, but also reflects your own individual style. Most cellars start out with at least a case of wine—twelve bottles—but start out with as many or as few bottles as you feel comfortable with.

Looking back at our original categories of wine, choose those which you personally prefer. To find bottles for ten dollars or less, look at the extensive Index of Common, Economical and Tasteful Wines which follows. Your initial investment could then be $120 or less.

Here are some of the wines you might choose. Note that there is, as usual, overlapping in categories. Many wines— such as Chardonnay, Cabernet Sauvignon, Chianti, Rioja, Zinfandel—range in style from simple and light to complex and full-bodied.

- Simple Dry White Wines:
  To be drunk within three to six months of purchase.
  Possible choices include Chenin Blanc, Entre-Deux-Mers, Frascati, Marqués de Cáceres Blanco, Muscadet, Orvieto, Pinot Blanc, Pinot Grigio, Sauvignon Blanc (or Fumé Blanc).

- Complex Dry White Wines:
  Can age one to two years or longer.
  Possible choices include Chardonnay, Macôn-Villages, Pouilly-Fuissé, Saint-Véran, White Burgundies.

- Aromatic White Wines:
  Can age one to two years or longer.
  Possible choices include Gewürztraminers and Rieslings from Germany, Alsace in France, California and Australia.

- Sweet White Wines:
  Can be aged at least one to two years, in some cases longer.
  Possible choices include Brown Brothers Lexia, California Chenin Blanc (off-dry), Seppelt Show Muscat, Vouvray, Sauternes.

- Sparkling Wines:
  To be drunk within three to six months of purchase.
  Possible choices include André, Asti Spumante, Bouvet
  Brut, Boyer Brut, Codorníu, Freixenet, Glenora Blanc
  de Blancs, Henkell, Lembey Brut, Marqués de Monis-
  trol, Willm Crémant d'Alsace.

- Rosé Wines, Blush Wines and Vin Gris:
  To be drunk within three to six months of purchase.
  Possible choices include Bonny Doon Vin Gris de Ci-
  gare, Grenache, Pinot Noir Blanc, Simi Cabernet Blanc,
  Tavel, White Zinfandel.

- Light Red Wines:
  The lightest, such as Beaujolais, are best drunk within
  three to six months of purchase. Some tannic Barberas
  and Chiantis need two or more years to be drinkable
  and can benefit from even further aging.
  Possible choices include Barbera, Beaujolais-Villages or
  Cru Beaujolais, Chianti, Dolcetto, Napa Gamay,
  Zinfandel.

- Full Red Wines:
  Benefit from aging at least three to five years; some will
  continue to grow in complexity if aged longer. Check a
  recent vintage chart or ask your wine merchant for the
  particulars on each individual wine.
  Possible choices include Cabernet Sauvignon, Chianti
  Classico, Crozes-Hermitage, Gigondas, Merlot, Pinot
  Noir, Rioja Riserva, Shiraz, Zinfandel.

Index of Common,
Economical and Tasteful Wines

Following is an index of some of the wines discussed in this book. Most of the wines below can be found for under ten dollars.

First is a list of some of the most reliable and consistent makers of simple jug wines. The important thing to look for here is the name of the winemaker or shipper; generic labels such as "Chablis" or "Burgundy" simply indicate whether the wine is white or red.

Next look for wines under their country of origin; remember that many countries use the same grapes to make different styles of wine.

If some categories seem sparser than others—for example, French red Burgundy—that is because the wine can seldom be bought for under ten dollars. But other categories—all varieties of American, Australian and South American wine, French wines from Alsace and the Loire and Rhône valleys, German and Austrian whites, Italian Chiantis and Spanish Riojas—are chock full of delicious bargains.

Jug Wines

Almaden
Barbella
Boucheron
Concha y Toro
Georges Duboeuf
Fetzer
Folonari
Fontana Candida
Gallo
Glen Ellen
Inglenook
Los Vascos
Paul Masson
Mirassou
Robert Mondavi
Monterey
J. Moreau
Raymond Pedroncelli
Partager
Principato
Carlo Rossi
Round Hill
Sebastiani
Seghesio
Taylor
M.G. Vallejo
Woodbridge

ARGENTINA

Red Wines

Cabernet Sauvignon
  Bianchi Particular
  Navarro Correas
  Pascual Toso
  San Felipe
  Trapiche

Syrah
  Navarro Correas

White Wines

Chardonnay
  Navarro Correas
  San Felipe
  Trapiche

AUSTRALIA

Red Wines

Cabernet Sauvignon
  Black Opal
  Brown Brothers
  Jacob's Creek
  Lindemans Bin 45
  Penfolds Bin 389
  Peter Lehmann
  Mildara Coonawara
  Rosemount Diamond
  Seppelt
  Wyndham Estate Bin 444

Cabernet/Shiraz
  Jacob's Creek
  Penfolds
  Rosemount Diamond Reserve Red
  Rosemount Shiraz/Cabernet Sauvignon
  Seppelt
  Tyrrell's Long Flat Red
  Wyndham Estate Bin 555 Shiraz/Cabernet
  Wirra Wirra
  Wolf Blass

Shiraz
  Brown Brothers

Shiraz (*cont.*)
    Hill-Smith
    Peter Lehmann
    Lindemans Bin 50
    Rosemount Diamond
    Rothbury Estate
    Seppelt
    Taltarni

White Wines

Chardonnay
    Brown Brothers
    Hardy
    Lindemans Bin 65
    Montrose
    Rosemount Diamond
    Rothbury Estate
    Seppelt Reserve

Rhine Riesling
    Jacob's Creek
    Penfolds
    Pewsy Vale
    Wynn's Coonawara

Sauvignon Blanc
    Brown Brothers
    Rothbury Estate
    Taltarni

Sémillon
    Lindemans
    Penfolds
    Rosemount Sémillon/Chardonnay
    Rothbury Estate
    Tyrrell's

AUSTRIA

White Wines

Grüner Veltliner
Gumpoldskirchener

Riesling (Krems)
Riesling (Rust)

CHILE

Red Wines

Cabernet Sauvignon
Caliterra
Canepa
Concha y Toro
Cousino Macul
Errazuriz
Los Vascos
Miguel Torres
Santa Carolina
Santa Rita Medalla Real
Santiago "1541"
Undurraga

Merlot
Concha y Toro
Errazuriz
Santa Rita

White Wines

Chardonnay
Caliterra
Cousiño Macul
Los Vascos
Miguel Torres
Santa Rita Riserva

Sauvignon Blanc
Canepa
Los Vascos
Santa Rita
Santiago "1541"
Undurraga

FRANCE

Red Bordeaux

Château Beaumont
Château Duplessy
Château Greysac
Château La Cardonne Rothschild
Château La Dauphine
Château La Grolet
Château L'Eperon
Château Larose-Trintaudon
Château Mauson Neuve
Château Roquefort
Château La Terrasse

White Bordeaux

Château Bertinerie
Martinon
Monsieur Touton
"R"

Red Burgundy

It is difficult to find true French red Burgundy wine for
under ten dollars, but check with individual wine stores.

White Burgundy

Beaujolais Blanc (Georges Duboeuf)
Bourgogne Aligoté (Aubert de Villaine)
La Forêt Blanc (Joseph Drouhin)
Mâcon-Lugny "Les Charmes"
Mâcon-Villages (Caves Talleyrand)
Mâcon-Villages (Georges Duboeuf)
St.-Véran (Caves Talleyrand)
St.-Véran (Georges Duboeuf)

Beaujolais

Beaujolais-Villages
Brouilly
Chénas
Chiroubles
Côte de Brouilly
Fleurie
Juliénas
Morgon
Moulin-à-Vent
Saint-Amour

Beaujolais Nouveau

Beaujolais Nouveau (Georges Duboeuf)
Gamay Nouveau (Georges Duboeuf)
Gamay Beaujolais Nouveau (Glen Ellen)

Sparkling Wine

Boyer Blanc de Blancs
Brut de Pecher (Corney & Barrow)
Crémant d'Alsace Brut (Willm)

Alsace Wines

Gewürztraminer d'Alsace (Domaine Lucien Albrecht)
Pinot Blanc (Domaine Lucien Albrecht)
Pinot Blanc (Trimbach)
Pinot Blanc ''Bergheim'' (Domaine Marcel Deiss)
Riesling (Trimbach)
Riesling d'Alsace (Domaine Lucien Albrecht)
Sylvaner (Hugel)
Sylvaner (Trimbach)
Tokay Pinot Gris (Domaine Marcel Deiss)

Loire Wines

Cler' Blanc (Sauvion)
Gros Plant Sur-Lie "Carte d'Or" (Sauvion)
Muscadet (Château du Cleray, Sauvion)
Muscadet Sur-Lie "La Nobleraie" (Sauvion)
Rose d'Loire (Château de Beugnon, Sauvion)
Touraine Sauvignon (Jean Sauvion)
Vouvray (Château de Montfort)

Red Rhône Wines

Côtes-du-Rhône (Domaine Andre Brunel)
Côtes-du-Rhône (Domaine du Moulin)
Côtes-du-Rhône (Guigal)
Côtes-du-Rhône (Robert Kacher)
Côtes-du-Rhône (Vidal-Fleury)
Côtes-du-Rhône-Villages (Domaine Brusset)
La Vieille Ferme Rouge
Parallèle "45" (Paul Jaboulet)
Sherry-Lehmann Maison Rouge

White and Rosé Rhone Wines

Côtes-du-Rhône (Guigal)
Fleur de Rosé (Georges Duboeuf)
La Vieille Ferme Blanc
Parallèle "45" (Paul Jaboulet)

GERMANY

White Wines

Liebfraumilch
    Black Tower (Kendermann)
    Blue Nun (Sichel)
    Crown of Crowns (Langenbach)

Glockenspiel (Julius Keyser)
Hanns Christoph (Deinhard)
Madonna (Valckenberg)
Meister Kronne (Langenbach)

Rhine Wines

Deinhard Riesling Dry
Forster Mariengarten Kabinett
Johannisberger Vogelsang Riesling Kabinett
Rauenthaler Baiken Kabinett
Rüdesheimer Berg Rottland Kabinett
Ruppertsberg Kabinett
Ruppertsberg Riesling Kabinett

Moselle Wines

Bernkasteler Badstuber Kabinett
Eltviller Sonnenberg Kabinett
Graacher Himmelreich Spatlese
Ockfener Bockstein Kabinett
Piesporter Michelsberg Kabinett
Scharzhofberger Kabinett

The 1990 Vintage 500-Milliliter Bottles

Carl Graff Riesling Kabinett
Schloss Wallhausen (Michael Prinz zu Salm Salm)
P.J. Valckenberg Riesling Kabinett

HUNGARY

Red Wines

Cabernet Franc
Cabernet Sauvignon
Eger Bikavér
Merlot Old Vines

White Wines

Gewürztraminer
Tokay Szarmorodni

ITALY

Red Wines

Barbera del Piemonte (Vallana)
Cabernet Sauvignon Trentino
Chianti (Frescobaldi)
Chianti Classico (Antinori)
Chianti Classico (Ruffino)
Corvo
Dolcetto d'Alba (Azelia)
Dolcetto d'Alba (G. Cortesi)
Grumello (Rainoldi)
Inferno (Rainoldi)
Regaleali Rosso
Salice Salentino (Cosimo Taurino)

White Wines

Bianco di Custoza (Zenato)
Bianco di Toscano (Antinori)
Chardonnay Trentino
Corvo
Est! Est!! Est!!!
Galestro (Antinori)
Orvieto (Conte Vaselli)
Orvieto "Campo Grande" (Antinori)
Orvieto Classico (Ruffino)
Pinot Grigio Trentino
Regeali Bianco
Vernaccia di San Gimignano (San Quirico)

Vino Novello

Cavit's Terrazze Della Luna Novello di Teroldego
Folonari Bardolino Novello
Giorgio Lungarotti's Falo Novello Rosso Dell'Umbria

Sparkling Wines

Asti Spumante

SPAIN

Red Wines

Coronas (Torres)
Gran Sangre de Toro (Torres)
Marqués de Arienzo
Marqués de Cáceres
Marqués de Riscal

White Wines

Ermita d'Espiells Blanco Flor
Gran Viña Sol (Torres)
Marqués de Cáceres Blanco
Marqués de Riscal "Rueda"
Viña Sol (Torres)

Sparkling Wines

Codorníu
Domecq Lembey Brut
Freixenet
Miro Brut
Paul Cheneau Brut Blanc de Blancs

UNITED STATES

White Wines

Chardonnay
  Alexander Valley
  Bald Eagle (Sherry-Lehmann)

Baron Herzog
Bridgehampton
Callaway "Callalees"
Dry Creek
Fetzer Barrel Select
Gallo
Haywood Vintners Select
Liberty School
Paumonok
Charles Shaw

Sauvignon Blanc
Bald Eagle (Sherry-Lehmann)
Baron Herzog Reserve
Dry Creek Fumé Blanc
Fetzer Barrel Select
Gallo
Groth
Robert Mondavi Fumé Blanc
Charles Shaw
Silverado
Simi
Sterling
Weinstock

Red Wines

Cabernet Sauvignon
Bald Eagle (Sherry-Lehmann)
Bandiera
Beaulieu Vineyards "Beautour"
Beaulieu Vineyards "Rutherford"
Estancia
Fetzer Barrel Select
Gallo
Golden Creek
Liberty School
Louis M. Martini
Robert Mondavi Woodbridge

Stratford
Windsor Vineyards

Merlot
Glen Ellen
Golden Creek
Inglenook Reserve
Louis M. Martini
Paul Masson
Monterey
Parducci
Sebastiani

Napa Gamay (Gamay Beaujolais)
Beringer
Fetzer
Glen Ellen
Charles Shaw
Weinstock

Petite Sirah
Louis M. Martini
Parducci
Joseph Phelps
Trentadue

Pinot Noir
Beaulieu Carneros
Buena Vista
Congress Springs
Davis Bynum
Monterey
Mountain View
Saintsbury Garnet
Seghesio

Zinfandel
Bald Eagle (Sherry-Lehmann)
Castoro
Caymus
"Clos du Gilroy" (Bonny Doon)
Fetzer Barrel Select
Louis M. Martini

Zinfandel (*cont.*)
Rafanelli
Seghesio

Rosé Wines, Blush Wines and Vin Gris

Rosés
Grenache (Almaden)
Mirassou
Robert Mondavi Woodbridge Rosé
Simi Cabernet Rosé

Blush Wines
Pinot Noir Blanc:
Buena Vista
Leeward Coral
Monterey
White Zinfandel:
Bandiera
Louis M. Martini
Mirassou
Robert Mondavi Woodbridge
Monterey
Weinstock

Vin Gris
Bonny Doon Vin Gris de Mourvedre
Sanford
Vin Gris de Cigare (Bonny Doon)
Edna Valley

Sparkling Wines

André
Ballatore
Domaine Chandon
Korbel
M. Tribaut Blanc de Noirs
Mirassou
Shadow Creek
Wente

Glossary

Acidity The amount of acid in a wine. While all wines contain natural acids, white wines are generally more acidic than reds.

Aftertaste The lingering flavor left on the tongue after tasting wines.

Age The time that wine spends maturing in tanks, barrels and/or bottles. Complex wines benefit from bottle-aging. Simple wines, on the other hand, should be drunk when they are young.

Alcohol The alcoholic content of wine varies from around 8 to 14 percent, with most wines falling somewhere around 12 percent. Alcohol, one of the principal components of wine, is a product of the fermentation of the grapes. Alcohol contributes to the taste of wine and also acts as a preservative.

Aperitif A drink taken before a meal to spark the appetite. Light wines and Champagne are examples of aperitifs.

Aroma The smell of a young wine. Not to be confused with bouquet.

Balance A harmonious agreement among a wine's acidity, fruitiness, sweetness, tannins and alcohol content.

Blanc de Blancs A white wine made from white grapes.

Blanc de Noirs A white wine made from red grapes.

Blush Wine A pale rosé made from red grapes. The most popular example is white Zinfandel, which is usually a sweet and fruity wine.

Bodega The establishment of a Spanish winemaker.

Body The weight, texture and alcoholic content of a wine. Wines can be light-bodied, medium-bodied, full-bodied or robust.

Botrytis cinerea Also known as "noble rot," a mold which concentrates the sugar and flavor of grapes. *Botrytis cinerea* produces the finest sweet wines in the world, including the French Sauternes and the German Trockenbeerenauslese.

Bouquet As distinguished from the simple aroma of young wines, the more complex aroma that develops with age in fine wines.

Breathing Some wines improve when you expose them to the air—that is, let them breathe—before serving. Oxygen brings out the full aroma and taste of wine. One notable exception to this is sparkling wine, which will go flat if exposed too long to the air.

Brut The driest type of Champagne or other sparkling wine.

Buttery A smooth texture and rich flavor reminiscent of butter. Used to describe some Chardonnays and white Burgundies. Characteristic of wines that are aged in oak casks.

Carafe The open glass container of house wine available at many restaurants.

Château In France, a house with a vineyard and winemaking facilities. The best Bordeaux wines are labeled according to the château by which they are made.

Claret The English name for the red wine of Bordeaux.

Complex A description of fine wines, reflecting their superior aroma and flavor.

Corky Smelling and tasting of the cork rather than the wine. A bottle of wine with a faulty cork should be sent back at the restaurant or returned to the wine store.

Crisp Describes wine that is fresh and lively, with a good acid balance.

Cru A specific growth or vineyard.

Delicate Light in flavor, fragrance and body.

Demi-sec The sweetest style of Champagne or other sparkling wine.

Depth Quality of a wine that has layers of bouquet and flavors.

Dry A term used to describe wines in which most or all of the sugar has fermented into alcohol. If the wine is extremely dry, wine experts refer to it as bone-dry.

Eiswein Germany's ultimate sweet wine, made from grapes harvested and

Shelagh Ryan Masline is a writer whose travels through Europe, South America and Africa gave her an opportunity to learn first-hand about the wines of different countries. Shelagh lives in New York City with her daughter Caitlin. Her previous works include books on health and environmental issues.

Vin Gris A pale dry blush wine made from red grapes.

Vinifera The species of classic European wine grapes from which the world's finest wines are made.

Vinous Of, having the nature of or characteristic of wine.

Vintage The year in which wine grapes are harvested. The date is useful to consumers for all types of wine; some vintages are considered better than others, primarily due to the weather conditions.

Vintage Champagne Vintage Champagne is made from the grapes of a particularly excellent year. Vintage years appear on the label of the bottle and are more expensive than non-vintage ones.

Vintners Winemakers.

Weighty Heavy on the tongue. Characteristic of rich, full-bodied wines.

Woodiness A flavor and aroma in wines imparted by the casks in which they are aged.

Yeast Natural organisms on the skins of grapes which cause fermentation. In modern wineries natural yeasts are often replaced with specially chosen ones to make the fermentation process more uniform and consistent.

Young In simple wines a desirable characteristic, denoting freshness and vitality. When used to refer to more complex wines, *young* means that they have not yet aged sufficiently to reach their proper balance.

Phylloxera A burrowing plant louse fatal to grape vines.

Robust Big and powerful. Even more forceful and sturdy than full-bodied wines.

Round The smooth and graceful flavor of a well-developed, full-bodied wine.

Sec A sweet style of Champagne or other sparkling wine.

Simple Refers to a straightforward, uncomplicated wine, as contrasted to a complex wine with multifaceted characteristics.

Soft In delicate wines a desirable characteristic, denoting a hint of gentle fruitiness. In other wines *soft* can indicate a deficiency in the balance of the wine, usually due to insufficient acidity.

Sparkling Wines Sparkling wines contain bubbles of carbon dioxide gas, which are produced naturally in the fermentation process or added to the wine. The most famous sparkling wine is Champagne.

Spritzer A concoction of a simple white wine with club soda and ice cubes.

Sharp Describes an acidic bite in some crisp, young wines.

Spicy Refers to the flavor and aroma of spices, such as cinnamon, cloves or pepper. Gewürztraminers are often called spicy.

Still Wine Wine that does not contain bubbles of carbon dioxide gas.

Sweet Sweet wines have a high sugar content. They may taste sweet either because sugar was added to them or because they were made from over-ripe grapes.

Table Wine Technically refers to any still wine that has not been "fortified" by the addition of brandy. In Germany this classification refers to a category of wine that is simple and uncomplicated.

Tannins Substances naturally found in the skins, stalks and pips of grapes, or added to wines through aging in wood. Tannins impart dryness and act as a preservative. Common in red wines and some wood-aged whites. If wines containing tannins are drunk too young, they may taste harsh and stiff.

Tart Refers to an overly acidic wine.

Vanilla An aroma and flavor of vanilla is often imparted to wines, such as Chardonnays, that are aged in oak casks.

Varietal Wines These are wines named after the grape variety from which they are predominantly made, such as Cabernet Sauvignon, Chardonnay, Pinot Noir, or Zinfandel. Federal regulations in the United States as of 1983 stipulate that a wine labeled as a varietal must contain at least 75 percent of the grape for which it is named.

pervision of a rabbi. Traditionally, Kosher wine was made from Concord grapes and was usually very sweet. In recent years, the selection of Kosher wines has become more varied and sophisticated, and includes a wide range of California, Israeli, French and Italian wines.

Labrusca A species of grape indigenous to the United States.

Legs Rivulets that run down the sides of a glass after swirling it, indicating that the wine you are tasting is rich and full-bodied.

Light-Bodied A wine that is light-bodied, or light, is low in alcohol and texture.

Lively Crisp and fresh, usually with a high acidity.

Maderization The name comes from Madeira wines, made on the Portuguese island of Madeira, in which wine is fortified with neutral grape brandy. However, it's also a process through which white wines, due to age or poor storage, become flat, musty and brown.

Mature A mature wine, in contrast to a young one, is a complex wine which has aged sufficiently to reach the proper balance—that is, it is ready to be drunk.

Medium-Bodied A wine that falls between light- and full-bodied wines, in alcoholic content as well as weight and texture on the tongue.

Muscadines A species of grape native to the American South.

Noble Rot Noble rot, or *Botrytis cinerea,* is a mold that concentrates the sugar and flavor of grapes. Noble rot produces the finest sweet wines in the world, including the French Sauternes and the German Trockenbeerenauslese.

Non-Vintage Champagne Champagne that is made from the grapes of a number of vintages, or years. More characteristic of the house style than vintage Champagne, and also less expensive.

Nose The term used by wine tasters to describe the bouquet or aroma of a wine.

Oak A flavor and aroma in wine imparted by the oak casks in which it is aged.

Oenophile (pronounced ee-na-file) A wine connoisseur.

Organic Wine Wine made from grapes grown without chemical pesticides and fertilizers. More American winemakers, especially those in California, are responding to consumers' health concerns by making organic wines.

Oxidation A process through which young and fruity white wine becomes stale, flat and brownish in color. Usually due to poor storage or over-aging.

crushed after they have frozen on the vine.

Extract Soluble solids from grapes that are present in wine.

Fermentation The process through which grape juice becomes wine. Yeast causes sugar to break down into alcohol and carbon dioxide.

Finesse The French word for "fineness," used to refer to wines of exceptional elegance.

Firm Describes a tight and well-balanced agreement among the different elements of a wine, notably its acidity, fruitiness, sweetness, tannins and alcohol content.

Flinty Often used to describe Chablis; a dry, mineral character; it is attributed to the soil in which the Chardonnay grapes used to make Chablis are grown.

Flowery Having the aroma of flowers. A characteristic of young or aromatic wines.

Fortified Wines to which brandy is added at some point to "fortify" them, or make them stronger, with a higher alcoholic content, than ordinary wines. The most famous fortified wines are Port and Sherry.

Foxy An adjective used to describe the unique flavor of American grapes, especially those from the eastern United States. Foxy grapes are said to be musty and "grapey" in flavor.

Frizzante The Italian word for semi-sparkling wines.

Fruity Fruity wines have the fresh, springlike flavor and perfume of grapes. Fruity wines are generally drunk when they are young, as their characteristics fade with age.

Full-bodied Full or full-bodied wines are high in alcohol and soluble solids from the grape, called extract. They generally need time to age, or mature, and taste weighty and substantial.

Hard Usually refers to a wine that has not aged sufficiently to achieve the proper balance. A harsh wine with pronounced tannins.

Herbaceous Refers to a wine that has the flavor and aroma of fresh herbs. Young white wines, such as Sauvignon Blancs, are often described as having a herbaceous character.

House The term most frequently used for makers of Champagne.

Hybrid Vines that are a cross between two grapes, usually American *Vitis labrusca* and European *Vitis vinifera.*

Jug Wines Simple, casual, uncomplicated wines. So-called because they originally were bottled in jugs. Now they come in all shapes and sizes.

Kosher Wine Wine made according to Jewish ritual law, under the su-

REQUEST YOUR FREE BOOKS!

2 FREE NOVELS
PLUS 2 FREE GIFTS!

KIMANI ROMANCE

Love's ultimate destination!

KROM15